THIS CHILD
OF
FAITH

Sophfronia and Tain

George Duncan

RAISING A SPIRITUAL CHILD
IN A SECULAR WORLD

THIS CHILD

OF

FAITH

SOPHFRONIA SCOTT & TAIN GREGORY

PARACLETE PRESS
BREWSTER, MASSACHUSETTS

2018 First Printing

This Child of Faith: Raising a Spiritual Child in a Secular World

Copyright © 2018 by Sophfronia Scott

ISBN 978-1-61261-925-5

The Paraclete Press name and logo (dove on cross) are trademarks of Paraclete Press, Inc.

Library of Congress Cataloging-in-Publication Data

Names: Scott, Sophfronia, author.
Title: This child of faith : raising a spiritual child in a secular world /
    Sophfronia Scott and Tain Gregory.
Description: Brewster, Massachusetts : Paraclete Press Inc., 2017. | Includes
    bibliographical references.
Identifiers: LCCN 2017041997 | ISBN 9781612619255 (trade paper)
Subjects: LCSH: Mother and child--Religious aspects--Christianity. |
    Children--Religious life. | Christian education of children. |
    Parenting--Religious aspects--Christianity. | Child rearing--Religious
    aspects--Christianity. | Gregory, Tain. | Sandy Hook Elementary School
    Massacre, Newtown, Conn., 2012.
Classification: LCC BV4529.18 .S393 2017 | DDC 248.8/431--dc23
LC record available at https://lccn.loc.gov/2017041997

10 9 8 7 6 5 4 3 2 1

Published by Paraclete Press
Brewster, Massachusetts
www.paracletepress.com

Printed in the United States of America

For Pastor Kathleen Adams-Shepherd
who remembers every child's name

CONTENTS

INTRODUCTION

Tain's nine-year-old face is calm despite the many film cameras and the super-bright lights illuminating the hallway of Newtown High School. My son has just completed the first audition of his young life. He's trying out for a new musical being produced by Broadway professionals that a Newtown father, Michael Baroody, brought to town for NewArts, a resiliency program he designed to use theater to help in the healing process for our community after the December 2012 tragedy at Tain's school, Sandy Hook Elementary. A documentary team learned about the endeavor and is filming the whole process. The director of the documentary, Lloyd Kramer, is asking Tain and the other children questions and enjoying the silly nature of their answers. He asks Tain, "What's the most important thing in your life?" I can see the slight smile on the director's face, and he and I both are expecting to hear a long list of the virtues of the Mario Kart video game or Tain's most powerful Pokemon trading card. Instead Tain thinks for a moment then answers with one word.

"God."

Lloyd's face freezes. He's stunned, speechless. He looks at me, but I hold up my hands in a "don't ask me" kind of way. He finally asks why, and Tain goes on to explain God's love and care of us, how God made the world. Tain says the words in a matter-of-fact way, without showing any doubt that each utterance is true. Why am I shocked? Because, as a parent, I can only do so much. I can model behavior, give Tain access to certain environments, tell him things. I can scatter seeds, but I have no way of knowing what has taken hold, what he will absorb and own for himself. Until that moment, I had no idea how firmly rooted Tain's faith was within him. For me it was affirmation with a capital A.

That was the spring of 2014. The documentary has become *Midsummer in Newtown*, funded by Microsoft co-founder Paul Allen's Vulcan Inc. and Participant, the company that produced the Oscar-winning *Spotlight*. It premiered in April 2016 at that year's Tribeca Film Festival and went into wider release and then digital formats (Amazon Video, iTunes) in 2017. Tain and I have done many press interviews (*CBS Evening News* and *Sunday Morning*, *ABC News*, the Associated Press, *BBC America*), and I noticed the journalists tended to focus on the same concepts and questions: *Tain's faith is amazing. You can tell it's important to him. You can tell it helps him. How did he get that way? How do you parent a kid to have such faith?*

I know they were asking because in all the screenings, the moment when Tain says "God" has quite an effect on the audience. I've heard gasps and felt a stillness fall over the room. That's when I realized it may seem as if my husband and I are doing something unusual, perhaps even extraordinary, in how we're raising Tain. I've been involved in Christian formation at our church for a few years now, attending workshops and teaching Sunday school for both children and teenagers, so I understand how some parents are at a loss as to how to help their children develop their faith. Sundays are taken up with sports and a host of other activities. The concept of Sabbath went out the window long ago.

And yet, parents know the concept of faith is important, even if they don't make time for it themselves. They sense it is the greatest gift they could give their children, but they don't know how to give it. Or they have a misguided notion about it; they think they can make random appearances at church or simply drop their children off at Sunday school to let someone else make it happen. But developing a child's faith is so much more than taking the child to church. Perhaps it's this "something more" that parents fear, because they worry they don't have it in themselves. They fear their own faith is wanting.

Tain and I wrote this book to shine a light on possible answers for parents by sharing our story. We hope our experiences will help parents get to the heart of a question that becomes more perturbing as our world grows ever more complicated. How do you help a child have faith—real faith, something he or she owns and not a regurgitation of something heard? How do you create a life space where a child can learn to understand what they believe?

But please note: this is not an instructional "how-to" book. As you'll see, we muddle along because there's no direct route here. It's as if God is a great secret I am dying to tell Tain, but I can't because I know it will mean nothing to him if I do. He has to discover God's presence and his own faith for himself, kind of like Dorothy in *The Wizard of Oz*. Tain has to know the home God has created for him lies within him and all around him.

To do otherwise would be like putting him in an arranged marriage, telling him he must be wedded to a belief he hasn't fully connected with on his own. He must develop his own love match, explore the depths of his own devotion.

Sections of this book will have "Tain's Take" on stories and portions of an interview he did with our Pastor Kathie, who was rector at our church during the time we're relating here. Tain was worried about what has already faded from his memory, but I showed him how the same tools I use in my writing to help me remember are all around him: photographs, pictures he has drawn, snippets he has written down that I've saved. He has no journal as I do, but I remind him he has the living memory of the people around him, such as Pastor Kathie.

Frequently in this book, you'll see various forms of *I don't know.* I mention this now in hopes that it will encourage parents who are thinking of not moving forward because they feel they don't know enough or feel they have to get their own lives right first. You'll see there are times when I'm flailing both in my faith and in my life, especially in terms of my vocation. All you have to do is step forward and sometimes, I've learned, even get out of the way so your child can lead you. Keep an open mind. Be willing to learn. And trust. Trust that what you need, whether it be people, words, or encouragement, will show up for you when you need it most.

Tain has had, at his young age, more challenges than many people experience in a lifetime. That's what made his response to the director that day all the more miraculous to me. How has Tain's faith endured, then, especially while the adults around him have had theirs shaken? As I said, this isn't an instructional book. But perhaps by showing you how Tain sees things, it will, as I know it has for me, help you see your life and the potential for your child in a more expansive way. The spiritual journey is neither straight nor perfect. But we are on it. And we walk it together. May you have the strength, faith, love, and hope to take up the path with your children.

THIS CHILD

OF

FAITH

CHAPTER 1

THE MOTHER AS CHILD

can't remember which I was aware of first: the light or the dark. I'm saying this up front because I don't want to deliver a false chronology, to have anyone believe that as a child I feared the dark and later found the light that relieved me of this fear. But really, I'm not sure if I could have made such a connection between the two. For all I know, writing now as a grown woman, wife, and mother, one who now understands fully how it is possible for a person to contain within herself paradoxes that must be managed on any given day, the child version of me knew of light and dark at the exact same time. I just didn't realize, perhaps, how they were connected—how one had the power to vanquish the other. But my spirituality does begin with how these elements existed for me.

To avoid this falseness and to honor the paradox I will first tell you of my sense of light.

The front lawn of my childhood home in Lorain, Ohio, is small and rectangular, and you can walk the length of it in five or six long strides. But in my earliest memories it felt like a grand meadow; to reach the street at the end of it was to meet the border of another country. The grass shone green like the colors in my picture books. I had six siblings, but somehow I managed to spend a good deal of time alone, often outdoors. I can only guess this was before I started school—which wasn't until age six—when my older brothers would have been at school and my younger sisters were too little to join me or, in the case of the youngest, were not born yet. This could also have been in the summer when I may have sought solitude and sanctuary from a small and noisy house. I would sit in this yard and play and survey the sky. One day, in the late afternoon, I saw rays of sunlight piercing the clouds. "Never stare directly into the sun." How many times had I heard that? My brother Wayne added a helpful detail—"You'll burn your eyes." I thought no one could ever really see the sun. So for me to see this sunray—to me a physical, visible, manifestation of the sun— was amazing! Who knew it was possible? I viewed it with wonder; no, not only that—I felt it. I felt it as a living presence, as if one of those rays could lay upon me something like a hand upon my shoulder. And I don't know why, but I had this sense that it would follow me everywhere.

Then the clouds shifted, and I couldn't find it again. But I kept looking for it and told my mother about it. And I remember the specific glee with which I did so, as though I'd made a new friend. I don't remember how she replied, but now that I'm a mother I know that when a child speaks from the heart the effect can bewilder and silence an adult. Especially after my younger sisters came along, I'm sure I must have kept my mom in a constant state of confusion because of the things I said to her.

But I remember that light. And I can say for certain, paganlike though this may sound, this is the seed from which my faith sprouted. It was no big step of reasoning to learn about God and to believe in his presence everywhere, because I already knew it. When we first went to church and I finally learned the name of this mysterious friend who came to me in sunbeams, the experience was more of a "Ah, that's who that is. Hello."

The dark came in the form of old copies of *Reader's Digest* that I would take from the waiting room of our family doctor's office. I liked the small size of the publication, how easily the copies fit in my hands. I didn't know these were shortened versions of stories that had been printed elsewhere. One day I read an article that made me cry. Well, that's putting it mildly. I was sad and frightened, totally beside myself all at once. The story told of a little girl who had cancer, and though I can't remember whether or not she had already died when the story was published, it was clear she wasn't going to make it. But what did it mean to die? The image I conjured was blackness—the dark surrounding me when I went to bed and all the lights were turned off. The dark behind my eyelids—I saw it as never-ending. I was horrified by the thought that one could be pushed away from life and put away like being locked in a closet. I didn't want that to happen to me.

So I cried. I cried and showed the article to my mother and told her I didn't want to die.

"You shouldn't be reading things like that," she said. She said I couldn't take it. This opened the door for me to think there was something wrong with me because I couldn't stop reading this story again and again, awash with fresh tears each time. *People die. Children like me die.* Nothing could console me or reconcile me to this devastating fact.

There was darkness and there was light. But I had no way of connecting the two. And because I saw the ray of light less frequently, while this story I read repeatedly, the darkness was foremost in my mind. I've since heard of other children who come to this same realization about death and become cynical and dark. Maybe it's a question of exposure—kids today see, hear, and read so much more, and a lot of that material supports their cynicism. Sitting through the six o'clock news offers plenty of dark fodder. Why didn't I become one of these children? Perhaps it's because

I had access to the possibility of the light—if not a complete understanding of it.

It's not as though my mother didn't have the answers. Her father, the Reverend Buford Stiles, was a Baptist minister who as a young man felt the call from God to preach Christ's word. He preached in the streets of Elyria, Ohio, sometimes from the roofs of parked cars. When I knew him as my grandfather, the man who gifted us with silver dollars at Christmastime, he was long retired from being the pastor at Mount Nebo Baptist Church. My mother said many times she had taught Sunday school. I don't know when and where she taught, but I would think this experience had given her the skills to help me wrestle with the darkness. But her response to my tears wasn't helpful. And even now, as an adult, if I look for help and find a resource unhelpful, I'm unlikely to consult it again. I probably never asked my mother about death after that.

But I know I must have some compassion for her. From my own experience as a Sunday school teacher, I understand that teaching a child how to look up Bible verses or build an ark of the covenant is very different from explaining how and why Christ is the light and his resurrection frees all of us from the darkness. Adults struggle daily to maintain their faith in this concept. My mother is closer to Jesus than anyone I know. In fact, she'll be the first to suggest praying to Jesus if you're worried about your car breaking down or traveling safely to a new destination. But I think my talking about death threw her for a loop. She is not one to engage in philosophical conversation. In certain ways her faith is childlike and no different from mine. She knows the sky is blue because she sees it. She doesn't need the details pertaining to color spectrums and the way our eyes filter light. One of her favorite songs, and she sang this to us all the time, was

> *Yes, Jesus loves me. . . .*
> *The Bible tells me so.*

And I'm sure that was the gist of it for her. The Bible told her so and she had no reason to believe otherwise. Her life reflected it. She had a home, a hard-working husband, and seven healthy children. She was blessed.

But how would I, a child, come to such an understanding for myself?

When did I make the connection?

I loved television. When I was younger it was black and white, and then one day my father brought home a console with a picture that was, to use the NBC phrase, in living color. What fascinated me about television had nothing to do with my favorite cartoons or sitcoms or police dramas (*Starsky and Hutch*, of course!). I loved patterns and routine. I recognized that what was on television in the summer was different from what was on television in the fall, when the new season began. I liked how there was a schedule, and if you knew the schedule, you could see certain things again and again—remember, this was the time before VCRs. On the weekend our local UHF station played the same film on Friday night and twice on Saturdays; that's how I consumed multiple viewings of fare such as the Beatles' *A Hard Day's Night* and practically every Jerry Lewis/Dean Martin movie under the sun.

This was also how I noticed and learned that the same films tended to be played at Christmas and Easter: *The Ten Commandments*, *King of Kings*, and *The Greatest Story Ever Told*. I watched them all, and I noticed that certain aspects of these films—the way people were dressed, the desertlike landscape—were similar to the pictures on the prayer cards I got from church, when we sometimes went to church.

Fairfield Baptist Church used to be a tiny white building near a set of railroad tracks in Lorain, Ohio. I'm not sure how long we worshiped there, but long enough that we helped care for the yard. I remember my father unloading the lawn mower from our car. He instructed my siblings and me in how to pull the weeds and the wayward clumps of grass from between the sidewalk cracks and around the row of stones edging the property. I remember the smell of grass—in the air when my father cut it, and on my hands when I pulled it from the ground. And I remember those little prayer cards and the colorful, fantastical images. I couldn't read yet, but I was deeply interested in these pictures. The colorful ones featured people wrapped in fabrics of bright blue, red, or green instead of regular clothing. The black and white ones showed images of angels with wings bigger than their bodies, and they were often levitating near or over some poor fearful and cowering soul. A few pictured a man with a dark beard, and in one he was surrounded by children. Another showed what looked like this same man, with nothing but a strip of fabric draped around his midsection, suspended on T-shaped beams of wood.

I mentioned Daddy: this is only a guess, but I think he was the reason we stopped going to church. I have flashes of memory of overheard conversations that tell me money may have been the issue. I think he resented tithing, handing over his hard-earned money, money further diminished when he retired with a disability in his late 50s and had to figure out how to keep our family of seven children (six of us under the age of ten) afloat on monthly Social Security and pension checks. I didn't miss church. Although I have no direct memory of the services, they must have involved some pretty fervent preaching, and people hollering and singing when they got the spirit. I say this because I've written two novels and both contain such scenes. They must have been imprinted in me somewhere along the line, and the impression, not a good one, stayed there.

Daddy didn't talk to us about God; he didn't have to. The Reverend C. L. Franklin (father of the famous soul singer Aretha

Franklin), Reverend Ike, and, at times, Billy Graham, did his talking for him. He'd play eight-track tapes of Reverend Franklin's sermons in the car and watch church shows on television on many Sundays. I wasn't usually watching the church shows, but our house was small so the words still reached my ears. Sometimes they preached what I think was the true message our Daddy wanted us to hear; he repeatedly played a spoken-word song by the gospel singer Shirley Caesar, a song that tells of a certain mother's two sons and how she lives with the wealthier son until he commits what we learned is the ultimate sin: he tries to put her in an "old folk home." The other son shows up in his raggedy car and offers his shabby home to her. Of course she's delighted to leave with him. I still remember the words sung at the end of the spoken part: *God gave you your mama. Don't drive her away.* They are seared into my blood.

Not until years later did I learn Daddy didn't know how to read. But even though I could read, from a young age in fact, he and I had this in common: we absorbed knowledge best through sounds and images. Maybe that's why I liked Bible films. In the movies the images from the church cards came to life. And I watched them because they seemed important—they were announced as "special events" in the days leading up to the broadcasts. I found *The Ten Commandments* more confusing with its cast of thousands. It was hard to tell who anyone was except for the guy with all the white hair and the long beard. The screen drew my attention when he parted the Red Sea. Before and after? I can't tell you. That movie had too much going on for me.

But in *The Greatest Story Ever Told* I liked the kind and gentle face of Max Von Sidow's Jesus and the big, sweeping landscapes and people looking very tiny moving about in this space. The booming soundtrack thumped in my chest. In *King of Kings* Jesus had incredibly bushy eyebrows and he wore red, which made him easier to pick out among the massive crowds filmed in so many of the scenes. The trailer for this film boasts of a cast of 7,000 for the Sermon on the Mount scene and refers to the movie's "surging drama."

Notice what these films left in me: impressions, mainly. I was too young to grasp the stories, let alone the theology. But I'm certain they laid the foundation for what was to come. I was primed to be excited when new made-for-television Bible movies premiered. *Moses the Lawgiver* and *Jesus of Nazareth*, both six-hour miniseries, had the same producer. (Lew Grade embarked on the Jesus project after Pope Paul VI praised him for the Moses film and encouraged him to tell the story of Jesus next.)

I connected more with the Jesus story than the Moses story—maybe from my old bias and boredom connected to *The Ten Commandments*. But it may have been more a matter of my age when I first viewed these films than the material itself. *Moses the Lawgiver* first aired in June 1975, the month before my ninth birthday, and *Jesus of Nazareth* arrived in 1977, when I was closing in on the age of eleven. The Jesus film changed everything for me. I could take in the words with greater comprehension. The images were just as striking—yes, the radiant blue eyes of Jesus, as played by the actor Robert Powell, enthralled me—people still write about this aspect of the film—but the story was so different. I didn't understand the political parts concerning Herod, Rome, and the Sanhedrin. But the things Jesus said in his teachings—it felt as if they were for me and not just the people he spoke to. I felt an immediacy, as if I had a role in this story as well.

"That which is born of the flesh is flesh. That which is born of the spirit is spirit."

"Be perfect, as your father in heaven is perfect."

"Give."

The words were important because they filled in the missing pieces. When looking up this film now on the Internet I learned there were a lot of people who, to Robert Powell's great ire, prayed to images of him in the role. I thought, "People, you're missing the point."

From the film, I learned that this man Jesus was a teacher, and that what he taught, while not easy to accept (he made a lot of people in the movie mad!), all made sense to me. Is someone in trouble? Help. Does someone have need? Give. Did someone hurt you? Forgive. Has someone angered you? Love. His teaching came not in a preaching voice—loud platitudes handed down from on high—but in what felt for me like real-life conversations with people hungry to understand how to live.

Please don't think the Bible didn't play a role. We had one in the house, bound in red leather, the kind where the words of Christ are printed in red ink. It had maps of the lands mentioned in the book, thin and colorful sheets of paper that slipped between my fingers when I turned the pages. But from *Jesus of Nazareth* I gleaned something very important that I was too young to cull from the Bible: how to be in communication with God. I learned how to pray. I learned that going off by oneself, as I often did, was a way of being with God. For years, the Lord's Prayer was the only pre-written prayer I found acceptable. I understood I could just speak and God would understand. "Your father already knows what you need before you ask," Jesus says in the film. This made so much sense I thought it more of an affirmation of feelings I'd only guessed at before.

The film even provided comfort for the question of death. There's a part where Joseph (the husband of Mary) dies and someone recites the lines "I went down . . . to the peoples of the past. But you lifted my life from the pit" (Jonah 2:7, JB).[1] These words, so poignant, made me want to cry, but even as a child I could tell these were different tears. They weren't tears of sadness and fear as I'd cried when I read the *Reader's Digest* story. These were the tears you'd cry when a parent or a friend shows up just when you need them—relief, gratitude, perhaps a hint of joy. Then imagine my happiness at hearing these words again, this time recited by the disciple John, outside the tomb as Jesus raises Lazarus from the dead. After he speaks the verse he says quietly, but with a tiny uplifted note of ecstasy: *My Lord! My God!* Tears in my eyes again. Yes. *My Lord. My God.* He will lift me from the pit. I was certain of it. (I eventually learned these words are from the Psalms, a few of which have versions of this expression.)

I didn't just take this comfort and walk off with it like Linus with his security blanket. In subsequent viewings, I figured out that following Christ was no easy thing. As I said, he made people mad. Even the disciples struggled with his words. Peter especially. He chafed at accepting Matthew the tax collector as a friend, but when he finally relented he said to Jesus, "Forgive me, Rabbi. I'm just a stupid man." But exchanges like this lent a reality to the events of the Bible that I never got from previous films. These were real people, with real concerns. When the pregnant Mary and a group of travelers were setting off to visit Elizabeth, a woman came running to give a package to one of the travelers with instructions to tell her cousin she would see her at Passover. Peter struggled with the choice to go with Jesus. He didn't drop his nets and walk away, seemingly in a trance, like the disciples in *The Greatest Story Ever Told*.

I didn't understand everything. "You must take up your cross and follow me": What does that mean? Is there such a thing as a child-sized cross? And where would I walk with it? At some point something will be asked of me. Will I be willing to give it?

This didn't come all at once. It came little by little as I grew older and watched the film again and again. It's interesting: when I was younger I related more to Peter. These days I am Mary Magdalene. More on that later.

The thin tract had a black cover with white type. I remember that detail but not the title, which by itself is a curious thing. I don't remember where I picked it up or what church or denomination had written and published it. The printed word fascinated me, so anytime I could lay hands on writing, no matter what it was, I did. In high school I subscribed to a religious news magazine called *The Plain Truth* because it was free and I was thrilled by the idea of getting new reading material in the mail each month, even though most of the content was dry.

Why do I bring this up now, this small collection of pages I read when I was a child? Because it held the missing instructions, or rather, the much-needed connection—the connection between the light and the dark.

In the beginning was the Word. . . .

Testified to the light. . . .

Here was the man I'd been learning about, and here's the thing I had to do: accept Jesus as my personal savior. This is how I would no longer fear death, how I could believe everything would be all right. Granted, there's a lot more to it, of course, because I still didn't quite understand the gravity of Christ's resurrection, but in that moment, as a girl, I found it was enough. And isn't that the essence of faith— to take what is presently given and run with it, knowing I would be provided with whatever else I needed along the way?

I found the tract. I said the words, "I accept Jesus as my personal savior." It was done. I felt it, I believed it. And my fear dissipated. I don't understand how; I just know it did. From that moment, for me, God/Christ and I were and are inextricably bound, his presence ever near.

From there our relationship grew. We went from the presence I felt then—and still do—in the rays of the sun, to ongoing presence.

And from talking to praying. I suppose that because I didn't know how to practice or explore this faith, it mirrored the connection to a physical parent, sometimes in the most earth-bound, human ways.

As a teenager, for instance, I would pray for my basketball team to win, and when we didn't, I would pitch a little hissy fit with God that basically amounted to my trying to ignore his presence and not pray. *Take that, God!* Thinking about this now, I probably needed to do this because there was no way I would have gotten away with a fit of any kind in front of Daddy. But the silent treatment, I learned, doesn't work with the divine—we always fell back into conversation, even a deeper one than where we left off.

In high school I read Dickens's *A Tale of Two Cities*, and to this day I recall the character Sydney Carton's contemplative thoughts on the night before he traded places with Charles Darnay and went to the guillotine. He repeated Christ's words, "I am the resurrection and the life. . . ." This promise seemed to be the reminder, the source, and then the strength he needed to make his sacrifice. He needed his faith to springboard him into the arms of the divine.

It seemed to me this is what you went to God for—the big things, not for basketball games. I don't recall praying for my college applications, and I suppose I also had a sense that God didn't concern himself with areas where I would be fine. Only in areas of need would my prayers kick in. Sometimes I felt I should be in a church worshiping formally, if only because I did feel this presence. I knew it was real, and I worried that if I didn't go to church I might waste the connection, like a talent uncultivated. I did try attending services.

In college, I thought about going to church. There was a beautiful church, Memorial Church, right there in Harvard Yard. And it had a kind, funny, gentle minister, the Rev. Peter Gomes, whom I liked very much, and who in some ways reminded me of my grandfather. But my first work-study job scheduled me to be behind the desk of Cabot Science Library on Sunday mornings. And I had experiences that made church a lot more complicated.

There was a large organization—these days it would be called a megachurch—in the Boston area; its members were both extremely nice and extremely enthusiastic about proselytizing and recruiting new members, especially among the thousands of college students populating the area. By nice, I mean they were quick to respond to smiles or even basic eye contact and engage strangers in conversation. Eventually they would ask about Bible study and invite me to go to one. I'd met these people on the subway, in stores, or while walking on the footbridge over the Charles River on crisp autumn days. It got to the point where if I met anyone who seemed friendly, I would check my watch to see how quickly we'd get to the Bible study question.

Usually these people, once they ascertained my lack of interest, moved on. But one year I met a guy—let's call him Max—who didn't disappear once I said no to Bible study. We met once for coffee, and I began to wonder if he was interested in really being my friend, apart from anything to do with his church. He and a couple of his friends, also from the church, helped me move into my dorm room.

At one point, and I can't recall whether this was later in the day after the move or on another day, Max was again talking about faith and Bible study when I came right out and asked him if my friendship was contingent on this. It was not as though I wasn't a believer. I believe in God, in Christ as my savior. Yet somehow he saw my faith as "less than" because I wasn't in his church. That bugged me, but that wasn't a deal breaker for our friendship. But the next thing he said was.

But first, to explain, let me introduce Kent. He was a classmate and remains a dear friend. He was a lighting technician, and we were both active in the drama club. I learned from him the language of lights and goboes and cues and filters. I had a fear of heights, so I was in awe of his ability to walk the grid where he hung lights high above the mainstage at the Loeb Drama Center. He had sandy blond hair and a love of mint Milano cookies and orange Poland Spring water, the fizzy kind. There was joy all about Kent—sheer joy in how he ate and laughed and spoke. The other day as I was watching the film *Finding Neverland* and heard J. M. Barrie, as played by Johnny Depp, describe Peter Pan as "the irrepressible spirit of youth," I thought of Kent. Even then I must have known he would stay this way, ever boyish, long after life happened to us. He also reminded me of Dickon from *The Secret Garden.* I could believe Kent understood how to make something grow.

One day he told me he was an atheist. I probably blinked once or twice while processing this information. I'd never heard of such a thing—how could he not believe in God? I was cautious in how I proceeded; I wasn't going to question him further. I was willing to roll with it—that was him, I am me. I guess I figured God would show up for him when the time was right.

Back to what Max said.

He said all nonbelievers go to hell.

Stop. Wait.

You mean atheists? I asked. All of them?

Yes. He seemed so certain.

You mean to tell me my friend Kent is going to hell? Everything about Kent made me certain he was one of God's more spectacular creations—a reminder of joy, of the potential of life, even an affirmation of God's presence. I'm supposed to believe God would toss Kent's soul into the pit? Wash his hands of him, as Pilate did with Christ? No way. God loves. God loves *all of us.*

Boom. Deal breaker. Max had lost me. Obviously, we didn't see God the same way. And over the course of our arguing this point it became clear to me that our friendship was indeed contingent upon me believing as he did. Sorry. Not gonna happen. I kindly showed him the door.

I thought most Christians believed as Max did. Christians like him give the impression that if you don't do certain things their way, such as making the proclamation about Jesus as your savior in public, going to their church, believing in the Bible to the letter, you are not doing your faith right. And who are they to say? The fact that they are insisting on their structure says to me they just don't get it. Hey, the Bible says, "Your ways are not my ways, saith the Lord. Nor your thoughts, my thoughts." And yet not only do they keep insisting on their ways, they insist their thoughts are what matters most, not God's.

Now here's the amazing thing, though, about faith and God. This experience could have put me off the idea of going to church. It has for so many young people. Why didn't that happen for me? Maybe because I had good signs drawing me toward the fold. Reverend Peter Gomes, for example. I wasn't baptized, and I had this idea that I would like to be. So, I made an appointment to discuss this with Reverend Gomes. There was a strange relief in having this conversation. He asked me about my relationship with God, and I told him I'd never had the chance to really talk about it—what I learned as a child, what I still found confusing, but how I had no doubt of his presence and participation in my life.

Then Reverend Gomes responded to what I'd said and what baptism meant. He confirmed what I had always sensed: baptism required something of me. A baptized person engages with worship, is active in community service, lives a life making outwardly visible the fact that they are marked as Christ's own. And Reverend Gomes spoke of commitment. I didn't have a place for that in my life. Here was the thing I wasn't ready to give. So, I thanked him and left his office. I was disappointed, but did I doubt my choice? No.

In my sophomore year at Harvard, I took a class in the Crusades. In my reading I found a reference to a saint named Sophronius who died in AD 638. Of course this piqued my interest, and I questioned the professor about it one afternoon. "Ah yes," she said, as though I had reminded her of something. "I noticed your name on the student roster and thought it was very curious. It is an old name, and it's not used much anymore."

She went on to explain that the "wisdom" and "sound mind" definitions of my name did not pertain to general knowledge, but a very specific one. "It's about knowing God," she said. "People over the years became uncomfortable with that idea, the concept of being close to God, of being able to know God in this way. So the name fell out of favor." I didn't know what she was talking about, and, to be honest, I still don't. The Bible is stuffed with direct interactions with God, and no one, to my knowledge, seems to take issue with that aspect of it. I have never seen any other reference to this idea of my professor's, not even in the vast ocean of information available on the Internet. I should have asked her to be more specific, to give me more background, more etymology.

I didn't ask those questions, but what my professor told me that day awakened a hope in my heart that said I need not worry. It was like a promise that I would one day understand this presence more. Simultaneously I felt comfort and confusion. Part of me wanted to indulge in a childlike satisfaction: I knew a secret no one else on the playground knew. But the other part of me wondered again about this gift and whether I could ever truly understand it. I carry this conversation with me still, like a darkened lantern waiting to be lit.

Can I say I was content in this? Yes. I was content for years. Every so often an encounter with church, at a wedding usually, discouraged me from attending services. You'd think it would be the opposite, but I had an impatience with sitting through the rituals. In my twenties I attended at least two Catholic weddings, and I remember being confused by the two decorated chairs set aside at the front. A friend explained they were for the bride and groom because the wedding service included a full Mass. I was raised on soap opera weddings that conveniently fit between commercial breaks. What kind of service was so long that the bride and groom had to be seated? Crazy!

My husband and I married (no seats for the couple required) in a Methodist church because that had been his father's leaning, despite Darryl's having been raised Catholic. When we moved to Yonkers after our marriage I found a Methodist church. I liked the idea of belonging somewhere and the routine of showing up there every Sunday, and perhaps that's why we attended just two or three times: neither of us felt that we belonged. We did this as something it seemed we should do, and I didn't connect it to my relationship with God.

So, when we had Tain, I knew it wouldn't be enough to just take him to church and tell him we have to do this. Something told me my experience of feeling God's presence so early was not unique, and that Tain, too, would sense something, have questions, would want to make connections. I shared my thoughts with my husband—that we should wait and take our cues from Tain when it came to religion. And so we did. But little did I know how much Tain's spiritual journey would affect mine.

Chapter 2

THE HAIRBRUSH SONG

How can I bring a child into this world, the way that it is?" I've heard that question so many times on television, in books, and in real life. This is not an irrational question when you consider the challenges in both your personal life and the world at large. In your personal life you think of time, finances, physical and emotional space, the strength of the relationships that will produce and support that new life. The world at large has limited resources, already taxed with the burdens of poverty, war, economic and political instability, and climate change. Why would anyone want to add to, as Ebenezer Scrooge called it, the surplus population?

And yet children are born. I can only think that for future parents, whether they realize it or not, whether they are religious or not, there is a leap of faith, perhaps multiple ones. My pregnancy with Tain required many such leaps, not as many as most. It was enough, though, to teach me something about faith. Perhaps this was even the first of many lessons about faith I would learn from Tain.

That I was pregnant at all was a shock and a miracle considering the condition of my reproductive organs in the late fall of 2003. I'd had a miscarriage a couple of years earlier, but that first pregnancy had been conceived so easily we assumed it wouldn't be long before I'd be with child again. But as months stretched into a year and then longer I knew something wasn't right. A series of tests showed a disheartening image I never thought possible: my uterus was scarred shut, a result of the treatment I'd received following the miscarriage. My gynecologist referred us to an infertility specialist, Dr. K., on the west side of Manhattan, and he performed surgery to remove the scar tissue. After a few weeks of healing I was supposed to start taking hormones and undergo more infertility treatment after I'd had a period. Only my period never came. We discovered I was already pregnant.

So I was already aware of miracle, and in the early weeks of the pregnancy I walked through the world feeling steeped in blessing. I knew the time of gestation is considered long—nine, really ten months (40 weeks), but I felt the time would melt in my hand like an ice cube and soon run through my fingers. I wanted to be present and enjoy every change as it came upon me. Those days were bright with possibility, and every little thing seemed different because of it. I craved the taste of salt, so I made rich beef stews to feed that desire. But for some reason my body suddenly found the scent of ginger repelling, a scent I loved so much I bought nearly every ginger product Origins sold—body scrubs, candles, and lotion. I laughed with wonder at such switch ups, and my hand would generally float to rest upon my upper abdomen even though there was no bump for it to rest on just yet.

Then one bitterly cold Saturday morning I found blood in my underwear. I didn't understand what I was seeing or why. My miscarriage hadn't been like this. I had gone to the doctor and learned my hormone levels had stopped rising and the pregnancy had failed to progress. I'd felt nothing, had no symptoms, had witnessed no signs. So what was this? I called out to Darryl. I told him we had to call Dr. K.

I remember Dr. K. asked, "What did the discharge look like?"

I did my best to describe the gradations of pinks and magentas and the stark red that had run down from within me.

"Is it still happening?"

"Yes."

"I'll be in the office tomorrow morning. We'll do an ultrasound and we'll have a look."

This wasn't an emergency response, nowhere near what I expected. There was a snowstorm whirling outside. I thought he was going to tell me the safest way to get to the hospital, how to staunch the blood until I managed to get there. He would tell me what to tell the attending physician, how long it might take for his own arrival. But I heard none of that. He told me *tomorrow*. An icy cold feeling settled over my body as I realized if he thought something could be done he would have told me all those things— but he didn't. I was losing the pregnancy and probably had to wait for the miscarriage to finish.

And then—darkness. There's the phrase from Psalm 23 about walking through the valley of the shadow of death, but that morning it felt more like a tube—a dark but translucent tube. I could see the world going on around me, and the tube was close enough that someone could walk next to me without realizing I was in it. But I knew I was in it, a tight place of sadness, unable to see to the other end. Inside the tube I tried to maintain the form and potential of a child I wouldn't get to know. I wanted this because I wanted something more to mourn than the flow draining from between my legs and because the sense of joy I'd had was once so tangible.

The next day at the doctor's office I lay there in the dark, Darryl next to me while Dr. K moved the sensor around within me. I tried to make sense of the fuzzy, wavy lines, but then I saw it: an amazing, pulsating drop of light, insistent and strong.

"There's your baby," the doctor said. "Normal, six-week growth; heart beating and everything."

Darryl asked some questions and Dr. K. answered them—I think he used the words "implantation bleeding" and "normal" but I wasn't listening. I just kept staring at the image on the screen. I was talking to it, saying to it in my heart where only he and I could hear,

I will never give up on you again.

For the rest of the pregnancy, I didn't worry about him—I anticipated him. I couldn't wait to see him. I wondered what he would look like. In ultrasound images I thought the shape of his head made him look like the little boy in the Ezra Jack Keats children's books *The Snowy Day* and *Whistle for Willie*. I bought these books for him, books I had loved when I was a child. From then on, everything was blessedly normal. Did I do anything to ensure it would stay that way? No, but I will admit to the one unusual thing I did—not that I think it had any effect, who knows, but for the curious here it is: every so often I would put headphones over my belly and play soothing music I thought he'd like—Chopin, some Beethoven—of course the Beatles, especially the song "I Will." I wanted him to know I'd love him forever, whether we were together or apart. Who wouldn't want to hear such a message? I don't remember where I got the idea to do this—I think I saw an illustration somewhere of a woman with headphones on her belly and I thought, "Hey, that makes sense to me!" I laugh as I write this because I know Tain, upon hearing this now, would give me that look of his, shake his head, and say, "Silly Mama!" And he would be right.

Yes, I anticipated him, grew big with him, shared my being with him as he began to kick and punch and turn. But then he was born early one morning at the end of July, via Caesarean section because my labor had failed to progress, and they put him in my arms at long last and I realized . . . he wasn't mine. I don't mean I thought he had been switched at birth. I mean: yes, I was holding him and in another few minutes I would be feeding him. But in no way can anyone claim ownership of such a powerful, singular being; in no way could I ever, ever possess this newborn star.

Today social and grammatical niceties require me sometimes to say "my son" or "my child" for the purpose of clarity and reference. But for the utmost clarity, know that I don't feel those words in a possessive way. Tain is, has always been, his own prevailing spirit, so big that I often feel the best I can do is get out of his way. He is himself. *And who am I?* I thought. I am—and I thought this with great humility and gratitude—I am the person blessed with the task of watching over him until he can make his own way in the world. My job would be to guide him and walk him through all the places he needed to go in order for him to become the person he would become. I prayed for help so I would know and accept this and decide accordingly, in Tain's best interest, whenever the important moments arose. I am Mama. Papa is Papa. This soul is Tain. He is Tain.

A word about his unusual name: when I was pregnant and learned I was having a boy I knew I wanted him to have an Irish name to represent my family's Scotch-Irish ancestry. I am black and both of my parents are black, but on my father's side of the family red hair and freckles run rampant. One of my sisters, preparing for a reunion, started researching our family background and this was her discovery. Who would have thought it was possible to be both black and Irish? I didn't! So I wanted the baby to grow up knowing this aspect about himself. But back then there were so many Ryans and Aidans (thanks to *Sex and the City*!), Colins and Connors. One day Darryl came home and told me he'd been listening to a jazz drummer, Jeff "Tain" Watts, and said Tain was a cool name. I agreed. It was simple yet different and elegant. We started considering the name, and I mentioned this to a dear friend who happens to be well-versed in Irish lore.

"Tain is an Irish name!" he said, and told me of an ancient Irish epic called *The Tain*. It's the story of a legendary cattle raid, and it has the same standing in Irish culture that Homer's *The Iliad* has in classical Greek literature. Tain means *cattle* or *bull*.

Obviously, I thought, this was supposed to be his name, and my husband agreed. Our son is Tain. And to this day that's how I respond when people compliment him or marvel over something he's done: "He is Tain." It is fact and explanation. His middle name is Elijah, another reminder for him that he is close to the voice of God.

I'm also aware of a certain dichotomy here. While Tain is his own person, his own being, there is the indisputable fact that he developed within my physical being, feeding off the nature of my blood and cells. I use that connection, both then and now, as a starting point whenever he has no words and I'm trying to understand what he needs. I think about my reaction to pain so I have a point of relation to connect with his. If I were too cold or too warm I would guess, until he could voice otherwise, that he was the same. When he was very young he seemed to operate with similar assumptions. He seemed to think he could eat what I ate, drink what I drank. I rarely consumed a whole of anything until he was about four. He took half of my chai, my soup, my apple, my broccoli, until he eventually decided he didn't like these things or preferred his own choices. Now he drinks hot chocolate instead of chai, and chooses spinach over broccoli; in fact he denies that he ever liked that vegetable.

Likewise, I feel the essence of faith is in our cells. But I don't mean this as something he inherited from me. In thinking about Tain's faith I simply recalled the development or recognition of my own, and I believed that he, like most children, would reach that point where he could form questions and make some sort of request. And because I was so certain of this I was comfortable with the idea of waiting for a signal from him about what to do about the faith question. My husband and I agreed we would take our cues from Tain and see how this path developed. This doesn't mean we thought he would suddenly get the spirit and start preaching (although we do have a baby picture of Tain with his Noah's Ark where he does look as if he's holding forth on the wages of sin) but he would at least ask questions. I didn't want him to think church was something in our lives only because "that's what our family does."

I know this was very un-Deuteronomy of me. And it may also look like a kind of abdication, or the kind of situation where kids run the household and get to choose where the family goes on vacation. Tain would be the first to tell you our family is not like that. But I do believe children can make inspired requests that come from a place of authentic desire or even divine guidance. They're not many—Tain has made two, maybe three at the most—and two of them you'll hear about in these pages. As the adults in charge we don't have to blindly follow through, but if we are connected to our children and know ourselves well enough to recognize our own right minds, we will be in a place to recognize the truth of it when a child speaks this way. Then we can act accordingly.

When Tain was four years old I enrolled him in a preschool, Trinity Day School, housed in a historic stone church, Trinity Episcopal, located on a hill in the center of town. I'd heard friends praise the school and had driven past it on enrollment days when its long, curving driveway was lined with cars filled with parents hoping their children wouldn't be turned away.

I didn't realize when I visited the school myself a couple years later that I'd lucked into a particular moment in terms of demographics. Not only were there fewer children in the system, but because Tain was starting at age 4 instead of age 3 and because I didn't mind

signing him up for the afternoon instead of the morning session, I
didn't have to fight the crowds to enroll him.

Why did I choose this school instead of one of the others in
the vicinity? I liked how the school was compact, just one short
hallway, but the building and its grounds were expansive enough
to feel like a small campus. They had an adorable grassy fenced-in
playground with a large wooden train to climb on, swings, and a
sandpit. It was vast compared to the tiny lot of toys at the daycare
where Tain had gone the previous year. The Trinity Day School
children also had the run of the church's large gathering room,
known as the undercroft, for indoor recess if the weather was bad.

But I admit, the detail I wanted to be sure of, the one I was
careful to ask about, was this: the school had no affiliation with the
church that housed it. It was not a religious program. I mention
this to illustrate exactly how far I was from thinking about religion
for my family. I didn't want anyone else introducing it or making
Tain feel it would be pressed on him before he was ready, before
he could understand that it was his own. I can only think my
wariness stemmed from my college experience with Max and his
determined practice of his faith. I know I was operating from a
place of mistrust.

Once I had my answer I could have left it at that and not
thought more about it. But come Christmas, I learned how much
I was wary of this affiliation. The children would be having some
sort of session with the rector in the sanctuary, and they would talk
about the crèche. I didn't know what a crèche was, but the frown I
get when I'm perturbed—the one where my right eye closes slightly
and my mouth twists up—wasn't about that. I was annoyed and
didn't understand why. I didn't say I wanted Tain to stay behind in
the classroom while the other children went. In fact, I made sure I
attended myself. I remember peeking in, seeing the low light of the
sanctuary and the woman in the clerical collar standing in front of
the children. She was talking about the nativity scene that stood

near the pulpit. The scene contained painted statues representing people, the kind of statue you might find in a yard display. The crèche, I learned, is the manger that the little statue representing the baby Jesus, which at that point was not yet present—and I didn't understand that either—would lie in.

I felt this had been harmless. Tain didn't ask me anything about it afterward, and it didn't seem as though the rector were telling the children they had to do or be anything. I was okay with it. Maybe I even thought it was something I could let slide. Did I speak to the rector? I don't remember. Tain knew Christmas had two ideas attached to it. He had only a surface familiarity with the story of the baby Jesus. Of course, Santa Claus is more interesting—and he brings toys!

If Tain had asked to know more about the baby Jesus, I would have answered. But his questions didn't start there. They came from a more difficult place.

Tain was 4 or 5 when he asked me why he had two grandmothers but no grandfathers. We were standing on a sidewalk in Washington, Connecticut, just before dusk, waiting for Darryl to bring the car from wherever he had parked it. I remember we were looking up at the first stars just appearing in a sky the shade of deep cobalt blue before it turns to black. He had a penchant for asking the unexpected question, but I wasn't ready for *that* question.

We had attended an open house for a private school we were considering for full-day kindergarten, because at the time the Newtown Schools only offered half-day. I'd told Tain the event was for him as much as it was for parents, and he could ask questions. We sat in a beautiful library and heard the headmaster and head of the lower school give their talks. When they asked for questions Tain raised his hand.

"Yes?" asked the headmaster.

Tain pointed to a piece of artwork on the wall just behind the man. "Who painted that picture?"

The headmaster blinked, then turned around and looked, his face revealing that bewilderment I mentioned earlier and for which I've developed such compassion. "I don't know, Tain," he said. "But we're going to find out for you."

I'd read somewhere that when children ask difficult questions you don't want to overwhelm them with information. The question may be huge, but their understanding, despite the mature sound of the question, is still pint-sized. You could overfill them all too quickly. So when Tain asked about his missing grandfathers I knew I had to walk a certain line. To say, "they both got sick and died," would have been too little, because children don't know the different gradations of illness. Tell a child that and the next time they get the flu they might think they're done for. Tain would need a little bit more.

I explained how both my father and Darryl's father smoked—a lot. Both of them developed an illness in their lungs and died, Darryl's in the mid-1980s and mine in 1991. Then Tain asked the obvious follow-up: They died? What does that mean?

"It's what happens to all of us. At some point we die."

"I don't want to die."

"No, but you are very young. You have your whole life ahead of you. It won't happen for a long time yet, and hopefully that goes for me and Papa too."

In that moment, this was enough, and he seemed satisfied. No need to talk of faith just then. It would have been too much.

That fall Tain did start attending the private school. It was 15 or 20 minutes away and started at 8 A.M., so we began the daily ritual of rising at 6:15 and leaving the house by 7:30. I would be there to pick him up at the end of the day. This time in our Subaru Outback station wagon each day was a gift—time for just us.

When I was pregnant, I knew exactly where he was; we were together and all seemed right with the world. Ten years ago, I was in San Diego promoting my novel. Tain was with me; he was only three months old. I remember taking a walk on a city street after being on the plane for so long. He was strapped to my chest in a Snuggly. I was thinking how complete I felt, that I had him with me and we were fine, healthy, and free. It was perfect, just perfect. He surprised me by starting to sleep through the night on that trip—such an unexpected gift.

I still notice that sense of wholeness whenever Tain and I are out together, especially in our car or minivan. I like looking at him in my rearview mirror and thinking that no matter where we're going, all is right with the world because he's there and I'm there and we're going somewhere together. It was heaven when I had my Miata and could have him sitting next to me. He loved that convertible as much as I did. He would tell me about school and we listened to music, often on a children's station on XM Satellite Radio.

Sometimes he would tell me about a song before I heard it. And, I will admit, if his description sounded outlandish, I wouldn't remember it. So one day when a song came on and Tain said, "That's the song, Mama! The one I told you about!" I wasn't sure what song he was talking about. But the song, which XM conveniently informed me was "The Hairbrush Song" by VeggieTales, was truly funny. I heard the quirky, clownish voice of someone called Larry the Cucumber, fresh out of the shower, bewailing the loss of his beloved hairbrush. "Oh, where is my hairbrush?" he asks. He eventually learns his friend Bob the Tomato is to blame: "I gave it to the Peach—because he's got HAIR!" *Nice hair, no fair!* Tain giggled as though our car's backseat were filling up with bubbles. I adored hearing him so happy, and we would listen to "The Hairbrush Song" repeatedly at home and on the road in the weeks to come.

Another day, at the library, Tain was browsing the videos in the children's section. "Mama! VeggieTales!" And indeed, there on the shelf were several titles. We saw Bob, a pleasantly plump and round red tomato, and Larry, a long, green, amiable cucumber. I learned these shows had just stopped airing regularly on NBC. "The Hairbrush Song" was part of the series called "Silly Songs," but most of the series had to do with telling kid-friendly versions of Bible stories. They covered Jonah and the whale, the story of Joseph ("The Ballad of Little Joe"), the Good Samaritan ("Are You My Neighbor?") and the Battle of Jericho ("Josh and the Big Wall"). Some, such as "Where Is God When I'm Scared?" talked about the nature of God in general. One video's songs even featured lyrics that said, "God is bigger than the Boogey Man and he's watching out for you and me." I thought that was awesome. The stories usually ended with a direct message from Bob the Tomato and Larry the Cucumber reminding children that they are special, "and God loves you very, very much." Okay, can I say how much I loved this? It's not enough to say I was thrilled. It just felt right—the right message, the right material, at the right time.

And I noticed this very important detail: Tain never asked me, "What's God?" or "Who is God?" I didn't question him, either, because I had the feeling that it must be like when I was a child— he already knew. Even if I did ask him I'm sure he didn't have the words to articulate what he knew, just as I didn't when I was probably about the same age. I knew this was okay. Here was the beginning; he was about to gain some purchase on something that was very much "out there" for him.

How would his journey take shape? It would be nothing like mine, I was sure. To begin with, he had no patience for sitting through movies, especially if they weren't animated. There was no way he would ever sit through a half hour of *Jesus of Nazareth* at his age, let alone something as unwieldy as *The Ten Commandments,* even only half-listening to it as I probably did. But these cartoons were brief—and funny! I enjoyed them, too, so I was pleased to start with this foundation. I would be watchful, curious to see what would grow.

Tain likes to listen to music while he's falling asleep. He would get "into" one particular CD and listen to it every night for months. Then he would move on to the next thing that caught his ear or his heart. Because of this I can almost mark the passage of time by what he was listening to. When he was very young he would listen to a CD of children's music recorded by our friend Francine Wheeler called *Come Sit Beside Me*. He heard those songs so much I wonder if her singing voice is still imprinted in him somewhere. Does that part activate when he hears her speak to him now? He's gone through stages of listening to music from soundtracks, such as *The Lion King* (both the film and the Broadway show), video games (Mario Bros.), and computer games (Club Penguin).

But at this time he was, of course, listening to VeggieTales. He had various recordings from the library, mostly from their "Silly Songs" collections. Sometime in 2010, he borrowed a CD that became his standard for quite a while: *25 Favorite Sunday School Songs*. It included songs such as "This Little Light of Mine," "He's Got the Whole World," and "Jesus Loves the Little Children." I was kind of surprised. These songs didn't have the humor and zing of "The Hairbrush Song." But I don't question Tain's tastes. That he can state a preference and show interest in any one thing is a good thing, an important thing. I allow and assist him in running down his current obsessions because this is the foundation for passion—it is practice for learning and pursuing what you love.

I've encountered many adults who can't tell you their interests, who don't know what they're passionate about. They float into whatever comes their way because they have nothing to weigh it against.

And I will admit this—I know Tain's ability to consume the same material over and over again comes from me. It's definitely imprinted in our DNA, because he would have been too young at this point to observe how I will watch the same movie, consume the same story, again and again. Now he's old enough to say, "Oh, you're watching *A Little Chaos* again?" in a matter-of fact-way. The wonderful thing about such obsession is I never know what will come of it. Sometimes it takes years.

So I was happy to run down more videos, DVDs, and CDs for Tain. He watched them all and knew their world as though it were his own. Even now, when I shuffle through the iTunes music purchases on my phone, inevitably a VeggieTales song will find its way into the rotation. He listened to the Sunday school songs throughout the day and at bedtime.

▪▪▪▪ Tain's Take

I used to watch this show called *VeggieTales*. It was a religious show about talking vegetables that would act out scenes from the Bible. I find it a bit creepy now, but it actually was the thing that made me start going to church. It started with one song from the show called "The Hairbrush Song." I heard it and then learned about the show and started to like it. It taught me about Bible stories like Joshua and the wall of Jericho, David and Goliath, the Good Samaritan—the list goes on and on. And after every episode, the tomato guy would say that God made you special, and he loves you very much.

I think that I liked this show because it was really funny. One episode called *God Wants Me to Forgive Them* was about forgiving. In the episode, these grapes called The Grapes of Wrath are mean to other people (really, they are asparagus) and to each other. The grapes are mean to a little kid and made him cry, and his dad comes out and tells the grapes to apologize to his son. They apologize, and the kid forgives the grapes. The grapes promise to never be mean again. The dad goes back inside, and the kid trips. The grapes laugh at the kid when he trips. The dad comes out and tells the grapes to apologize and they do. But the kid doesn't forgive them. He says that they will never be nice so he won't forgive them. But he then learns that God wants you to forgive people all the time. So the kid forgives them and the grapes become nice grapes. This episode taught me about forgiveness.

I eventually asked my mom who God is and what Sunday school is. She thought this was a strange question from me. But because of this question, she decided that we should go to church. And it was all because of that one song.

Eighteen months into our VeggieTales adventure, one night I was putting Tain to bed and turning on his CD player so he could listen to the Sunday school songs as he fell asleep, and he asked the question—*the* question.

"Mama, what is Sunday school and can I go?"

My head popped up in a light-bulb-moment way. I answered him brightly, quickly, without a moment's hesitation. To think about it now, I'm surprised I answered so fast—it was as if the words had been waiting, perhaps waiting since he had been born, to roll out with joy and wonder.

"Tain, that's a great idea!" I said, and I threw up my hands. "We'll all go! You, me, and Papa—we'll all go!"

Granted, I still had that sense of mistrust somewhere inside me. I would have to handle it, overcome it, do *something* with it, and I didn't know what that would look like. I only knew Tain was voicing the big request—even bigger than he realized. And I would respond. I told him I would start looking for a place for us to go to Sunday school. I promised we would go.

Chapter 3

THE SEARCH FOR
A SPIRITUAL HOME

First of all, let's address the elephant in the room: why would I want our family to go to church when I never connected with a church myself? I still didn't know the differences among the various Protestant denominations, and I only had a handle on the difference between Catholic and Protestant thanks to history in school, including a college course on the Crusades. (By the way, that class was my first education on the dark side of faith and how it can be used for terrible purposes. It bewildered me, to say the least.) I also think I had more of my father acting in me than my mother. Daddy would be more likely to think about what the people in the church would want from him. Not that he wasn't willing to give it, but would he be able? He was a good caretaker, and even as a child I noticed how people depended on him for advice, to fix things. He was aware, I think, of his resources both financial and emotional.

My mother, on the other hand, can still enter any church and find herself at home because she is in Jesus's house. But then, I liken her to a superstar athlete who also happens to be a terrible coach. She does what she does so instinctively when it comes to her faith that she can't impart the information to others. So I couldn't ask her how to go about the search although I would have liked some of her confidence. When I look back on how I conducted the search, however—how little in the way of hard research I actually did—perhaps I ended up behaving more like my mother after all.

This surprises me. I'm originally a journalist by trade, and the first thing I learned as a new reporter was how to research any subject, both pre- and post-Internet. So why wasn't I on Google looking up churches, reviewing their websites, studying photos of congregations? I can only guess that I didn't know what to look for, plain and simple. I didn't know what questions to ask. I assumed all churches had Sunday school and that all Christian belief was pretty much the same, though perhaps not at the Max-like intensity level.

But back to the initial question: Why even try? My answer is simply this: structure. Tain was six years old when he asked about Sunday school, and by this time I had observed how routine and structure were helpful and comforting in many areas of his life: bedtime, getting ready for school, meals. Over the years the details of his routines have changed, but the core of them remains. He has never liked to be rushed and prefers to waken forty-five to sixty minutes before he has to leave the house for school or any other morning event. He drinks hot chocolate every morning. It's gone from being made with Hershey's chocolate syrup to Swiss Miss cocoa mix, but it's always made with milk (unless he's on a Boy Scout campout; then it's water) and he drinks it from a go cup, these days a reusable one he bought himself from Starbucks. When we're on the road, the hot chocolate can be served at a diner or a Starbucks or, his preference, Dunkin' Donuts. In the evening, Darryl is almost always the one who tucks him in. They used to read together and then turn on Tain's music for him to listen to as he fell asleep. These days Tain goes upstairs on his own, and once he's brushed his teeth and cleaned up, they talk instead of read, and Tain listens to Harry Potter audiobooks once the lights are out.

I like that Tain has managed to adjust with age, how it's okay now if some aspect of his routine can't be done because we're traveling or some other reason. He knows he can't be attached to what can easily change. So I'm comfortable with offering him church however it may look. I know he will hold it lightly. I know it will not consume him. Besides, I don't think about structure in terms of rigidity. Structure provides a safe space in which to explore. I believe if a child knows certain factors will remain the same, they will be freer about introducing variables and playing with the unknown. If my husband and I could provide Tain with the right routine and the structure of church, he would be comfortable exploring his faith and have a natural place to ask questions. And since this new family practice was Tain's idea, I knew he would take ownership of it and always know for himself why we were going to church.

My husband and I agreed the choice of when and how to fulfill Tain's request would be mine. Darryl is a lapsed Catholic with strong Buddhist tendencies, but he supported my quest, and this has been important. Many children attend church with only one parent (or on their own), but I wanted Tain to have the unity of our family supporting his faith. I also suspected the long-term success of any family endeavor would be compromised if it weren't buoyed by the participation of both parents. Otherwise inevitably the questions would arise: "Why does Papa do that and not us?" or "Why doesn't Mama go to X with us?" Seeing opposing narratives, usually the child eventually comes to feel he must choose one or the other—and I think a lot of teenagers probably choose based on convenience. I could see that easily happening if we didn't all enter this new experience together.

Being in agreement on something as big as figuring out our family's faith life was huge, and I appreciated Darryl's willingness. He easily could have opted out, and he has no qualms about exercising that freedom. So, I was glad Darryl and I were on the same page, and I wanted to honor his flexibility by making sure I chose a church that was acceptable to and comfortable for him. He didn't offer suggestions, but I knew what would be deal breakers. He wouldn't tolerate music he didn't enjoy, which would include a lot of contemporary Christian music. No testifying, no speaking in tongues, no sermons that didn't go anywhere. Well, anyone can deliver a clunker once in a while, but Darryl wouldn't endure a weekly diet of such fare. I could agree with him on all these points, so I wasn't worried that I would like a place he didn't.

Our local newspaper, *The Newtown Bee*, features a weekly religion section listing the multitude of area churches along with contact information, locations, and service times. I started there, noticing right away the name of a minister I'd met when we had served on a school committee together. His church, he'd told me in past conversations, was fairly new and small; it shared space with another church, using their sanctuary later on Sunday. It seemed easier to begin where I knew someone, so I attended a service there.

The minister greeted me warmly. He asked about Tain and explained how the children would be taken downstairs via a door at the front of the church for their own service and Sunday school. I said I hadn't brought him. I didn't explain I was church shopping and didn't want to bring Tain until I was sure where we wanted to be. When I moved through the pews to choose a seat I sensed a spark of anticipation, like a small tug in the center of my belly, and I realized the feeling was not unfamiliar. I have always felt hopeful when sitting down in a church. What was I expecting, then and now? I don't know. Maybe I find the wide-open sanctuaries cheerful and inviting. Maybe I sense the frequency of prayers upon prayers spoken over many years in that space. Maybe it is the books placed in the holders in front of me—hymnals and often Bibles, depending on the church. As a child I remember being excited by the books, thinking they were free and asking if I could take them home. Surely, recognizing this hopeful feeling in that moment meant I was supposed to be in a church somewhere. Would it be this one?

But I had a conflicting thought working on me too. What was behind that door up front on the right, the one the children would go through at the start of service? It bothered me that I didn't know, and if Tain were with me I would not have sent him out that door. I could find out, though, right? If I liked the service I could ask to see where the children learned and prayed. I could get familiar with it. I knew this was a logical thought. So why did I feel conflicted?

The service began and I picked up the hymnal. I didn't sing—I looked at the words and listened. Thinking about that now, it feels as if I was holding back, as though if I began to sing I would be offering some sort of tacit agreement. Strange thinking, yes, but there it is. I picked up the Bible. I can't remember when or how I learned how to find chapters and verses in the Bible. I probably figured it out for myself, and not very well, because back then every time I picked up a Bible I felt that I had to recall how to do it again.

A side note: I did own a Bible. I had bought it in college when I was searching for textbooks at the Coop bookstore at Harvard and came across the shelves of required reading for a religious studies course. I saw the Bibles and felt drawn to pick one up. It was medium-sized, a little larger than a regular paperback, but with a hardcover, black. I wanted it. I don't know why. Perhaps the maps on the end papers reminded me of the Bibles I'd thumbed through as a child. Maybe I was drawn to the poetry of it: this was a King James version, which remains my favorite translation, though my main reader copies now are NRSV. The elegant wording in Genesis grabbed me right off the bat: "And the evening and the morning were the first day" (Gen. 1:5). I bought the Bible, wrote my name in the front, and dated it so I can tell you accurately that this was in

September of my senior year. I read some of it—pieces of the New Testament, most of Genesis and perhaps some of Exodus as well, and that was it. I liked having it, though. I like that I still have it.

Certain things about that service stayed with me and others didn't, and I believe that mix is what affirms for me that I made the right choice in not attending the church. The hints of fundamentalism (though I didn't know then that's what it was) were there; the music—contemporary Christian—was okay but left no impression; the same thing goes for the sermon. It was friendly, outgoing, relating to one of the Bible passages read that day, but I'd written nothing down, and the words left me after I'd heard them.

But the time of public prayer (my words, I don't remember what their term was for it) did stay with me. The people stood and spoke, and the stories were sad—stories of trial, stories of sickness and of lack. I don't remember them, not that they would be mine to tell, but I remember feeling as though I were in a hospital. And we prayed, but I felt no power in that prayer. No agency. Instead, I felt as though I were stepping back within myself. Don't get me wrong— they had come to exactly the right place for intercession. We are all broken, and it wasn't the brokenness that kept me at arm's length. It was the focus on the brokenness. It was the focus on the weight of sin and falling short of God's love. Faith is so much more.

I believe in light. I believe in possibility. I believe in God's unshakable, enduring, gracious love for me. Marianne Williamson was right in that famous quote of hers: "You are a child of God. Your playing small does not serve the world. . . . We are all meant to shine, as children do. We were born to make manifest the glory of God that is within us." I think when a person is a certain way, carries himself a certain way, the world can't help noticing and becomes curious about the source.

There's a story in *Harry Potter and the Deathly Hallows* that tells about when Harry gets to witness his own father as a boy traveling to wizard school for the first time. I find this intriguing because of the description of James in comparison with an unfortunate boy, Severus Snape, as having "that indefinable air of having been well-cared for, even adored, that Snape so conspicuously lacked."[2] I believe in carrying myself this way, as a child of God, walking in the knowledge of grace, confident that I'm beloved and well cared for. I focus on joy, on an abundance of love. That doesn't mean I'm not broken; it does mean I think about the possibility of being whole.

I can embrace the knowledge that I am truly loved because this is in alignment with the feeling I had as a child. I remember one beautiful, sunny morning when I was about five years old, and my mother had me and four of my siblings out in the front yard trying to take our picture. (My oldest brother, age 14, was at school; my youngest sister was not yet born.) The scene was chaotic, because my mother couldn't get us to stand still at the same time; we were running all over the yard. There's my brother Wayne, age 7, who was supposed to be home sick but was outside in his pajamas. There's me, there's my sister Theodora, age 4, my sister Denise, age 3, and my sister Jeanette, age 1.

I remember that day so clearly because I remember how I felt: happy to be in front of the camera, joyously pretending I was Miss America and posing as if I were. I remember acting as if I was the most beautiful girl in the world, because that's exactly what I believed. Yes, I probably looked like a well-loved child. Nearly all of the photos my mother took that morning were destroyed in a fire, and for years I had forgotten they existed. Then, during a visit home I happened to find a scorched Polaroid. In this photo I was airborne; the photo caught me mid-skip or mid-jump. I was laughing.

I remember how I felt that day—that I was loved and I loved myself. Somewhere along the line that feeling, dampened no doubt by puberty and all the insecurities that went along with it, had been taken away from me. I told myself I would never allow that to happen again. I made a copy of that picture, and I keep it here in my home to this day to help me remember that this is who I am by nature. I may forget from time to time that I am loved. I may grow insecure about who I am. But coming back to that knowledge, embracing it, is no difficult process because it is my foundation. I welcome the feeling with happy tears, just as I would welcome the return of an old friend.

Yes, there is suffering, and being a human is difficult, but do those aspects have to hold sway so much of the time? Once, at a lecture on gratitude, I was struck by how many of the situations people shared were about coming to a place of gratitude through pain and loss. I understand how such pain can provide a crack through which the light of God shines. But I also firmly believe it isn't the only way God can reach us. I am always hugely aware of when and where I am *not* suffering—and those places where I am not suffering outweigh the areas where I am. This isn't always the case, but that's the way it has worked for me. Here's an example: I have had two miscarriages, and I haven't been able to get pregnant again despite repeated surgeries and fertility treatment. I could be suffering over that in every which way (and there are times in the past when I did), but how can I continue in that mode when I have Tain? Yes, I would love to give him a sibling—I think that's one of the greatest gifts any parent can give a child. But he is an amazing boy and we are blessed to have him. I accept that he was probably meant to benefit from our sole focus, and I see him flourishing from it. Bad things happen; some might think my family has had more than the norm. We can find our way into gratitude in those times, but it doesn't have to be only way we find gratitude. The world is not set against us. I truly believe that.

Why is this important? On the surface, it might sound as though I'm saying, "Oh, this church is a drag, I want one that's more fun," but it's really about this: I believe that how you carry yourself is one of the most powerful ways you demonstrate what it means to be a follower of Christ, to know the good news. As the quote often attributed to St. Francis goes, "Preach the gospel at all times, and if necessary, use words." I understand the importance of this more and more as Tain grows, and I can see how he influences people simply by the way he is in the world. I'll say more about this later. For now, know that as I looked for a church I wanted to feel an embrace and at least some acceptance of God's love. I wanted that feeling to be the foundation on which Tain could stand and grow in his faith. It made no sense to me to bring him to a place where he might experience what I had experienced with my mega-church friend at college: that God was for some and not others, that if you didn't accept Jesus Christ in exactly their way, your belief didn't count. And it's not just that I didn't want my child in that environment—I think it wouldn't have made sense to Tain. He would recognize this didn't fit with his expansive feeling of God. VeggieTales had told him, after all, that God was bigger than the bogeyman.

The gift of this visit was my recognition that I wasn't looking just for Tain's sake and to satisfy Darryl. Something in me wanted to put down roots in the right place. Some aspect of me wanted to come to new life. So instead of feeling I would always be disappointed or dissatisfied with church, I was ready to continue looking. Something must have made me feel the right place was out there somewhere despite my never having experienced it or even been able to articulate what I was looking for.

On my way home I drove past the old stone church at the top of the hill where Tain had gone to preschool. It's hard to miss it.

Trinity is close to the flagpole planted smack dab in the middle of Route 25, our Main Street, in the center of town. When illustrations of the town are depicted, Trinity is usually included— part of Newtown's "skyline." Maybe that familiarity is a virtue, I thought. Tain might recall going to school in the building, and I had a basic knowledge of at least one floor of Trinity. I thought about how my friend Francine was already going to church there with her sons, both dear friends of Tain's and close to him in age. But what was this church? I knew Francine was Catholic, so there must be some aspect of that faith there, I assumed. Trinity wasn't Catholic, though. I decided to look further into the stone church on the hill.

I visited Trinity during the week at a time when Tain was at school. I parked on Main Street, by its front. At the time I thought the back doors were for the preschool, so I approached the church's large red doors.

When I was a girl I read the book *Escape from Witch Mountain*, in which a girl named Tia could open any locked door simply by turning the handle. It only worked if it was okay for her to be in there, a right place to be, such as a library or a church. She could not open doors where she had no business being, such as a bank to steal money. That aspect of the story has stayed with me. Like any kid today worth his or her Harry Potter salt, I was enchanted by the prospect of having such a magical power. But even more so I felt comforted by the idea that safe places would always be open and available. That's the way I wanted the world to work. I understand churches must be locked these days because of theft and safety issues. That doesn't keep me from feeling a tiny pinch of disappointment whenever, in my travels, I come upon a beautiful church and want to enter but find it locked. The fact that Trinity's bright red doors opened for me that afternoon was a good sign.

Once inside I could see why those doors could be left unlocked, and I appreciated the design. The glass doors leading into the sanctuary were locked, and a large wooden door to my right, which I assumed led to another part of the church, was locked as well. But to my left I could enter a tiny chapel furnished with chairs and kneelers in front of a small altar and a cross. It had a stone floor and a fleur-de-lis pattern on the frosted windows. Wooden holders on the back of each chair held a Bible. This made so much sense. Someone could come in for quiet, privacy, and prayer at any time while the rest of the church remained safely locked.

I returned to the dimly lit foyer. The doors to the sanctuary were flanked by two white statues of saints, each about four feet tall. I peered through the glass, and a few of the stained-glass windows were catching the sunlight, their colors reflected on the floor and walls—ruby red, sapphire blue, emerald green. Over the altar was a giant stained glass window with a picture of Jesus wearing a white robe and a bright red sash. His arms were stretched upward, much as a toddler would do while waiting for a parent to lift him. The ceiling over the stained glass was painted sky blue, and I could just make out gold stars decorating this firmament. I eventually learned the portrait does indeed depict Christ's ascension.

In the foyer there was a small wooden case on the wall filled with tracts; I picked a few up and, standing there, began to read them. These tracts, published by Forward Movement, an organization described on the back of each piece as "an official non-profit agency of the Episcopal Church" weren't like the one I'd seen in childhood, outlining precise instructions on how to be saved. Instead, the titles and illustrations felt friendly and already informative:

The Episcopal Church Welcomes You
Why I Am Now an Episcopalian
Belonging
Raising Children of Faith

To start, what is the Episcopal Church? I could have stopped reading it at the first two sentences, the words felt so right:

"The Episcopal Church owes its foundation to Jesus Christ. It is organically related to the Church of England." I am something of an Anglophile—I've been one since childhood, when I had a mad crush on the little English boy Jimmy, played by Jack Wild, in my favorite Saturday morning television show, *H.R. Pufnstuf.* My favorite books in high school had been nineteenth-century British authors—Austen, Bronte, Dickens—and I set my alarm so I could wake long before the rest of my family and witness the wedding of Prince Charles and Lady Diana. I had also studied the history of England, so I knew about Henry VIII and the origins of the Church of England. The Episcopal Church even had its own coat of arms. Silly, I know, but I'm being honest: these details piqued my interest.

The tract went on to explain, "Our tradition is a blending of evangelical and catholic (Eastern and Western) Christianity in which Christians of all traditions may find a home and where each tradition enriches and fulfills the others." To me this meant here was a place where Darryl might feel comfortable, where the Buddhist aspects of his spirituality would not be affronted.

"What is the faith of the church?" it asked, and answered, "Christian doctrine, as taught by Anglicans, must conform to three criteria: scripture, tradition, and reason." All this made sense to me, especially for Tain. I wanted him to feel at ease with reading the Bible and engaging with its contents. Tradition would provide the structure I sought for him, and the reason part to me meant that he would be encouraged to think about his faith—to ask the questions he would no doubt ask now and in the years to come.

I was happy with all of this, but then I opened Lawrence D. Hart's explanation of why he had become an Episcopalian and found words I never thought possible—words that described my experience of God, from that first moment in the front yard of my childhood home.

I have found a tradition that encourages the cultivation of the inner life and that believes in a direct encounter, an experiential knowledge, a mystical union of love with the divine mystery we know in scripture as the God of Abraham and Sarah, of Moses and Miriam, of Mary, and Paul and Phoebe and, of Jesus—the God who is warmly and profoundly personal.

Yes! I stood there in the foyer and if someone had walked in then they would have thought me off-kilter because I was whispering to myself, *Yes, yes, yes.* This was how I believed! I know it may not make sense or even sound humble, but I had gotten to a point in my life where I didn't believe I would find a church where my particular spirituality would feel at home. The mysticism part was a little over my head, but what it described did feel familiar: the concept of being in personal relationship with God, to desire to seek and feel his presence. This is what I'd been doing all along from the very moment I saw those sunrays as a child and knew I wasn't alone.

The joy I felt at that moment made me realize I had embarked on this search with no hope of complete success—I had been seeking an approximation, something we could live with, something that wasn't imposing. But isn't that how God works? I set out seeking something "less than" and here God showed me I could have "more than." To me this was a tiny example of that very large notion Oprah Winfrey likes to point out: "God can dream a bigger dream for you than you could ever dream for yourself." Was the Episcopal Church my bigger dream?

I read one more—the "Raising Children of Faith" tract. It offered "six important concepts that guide us in raising children of faith" and they were all good—concepts such as "Children need to know the Christian stories" and "Children need to know that God loves them." But I felt deeply connected to these two sentences from the introduction:

Then, there are all the spontaneous teaching moments that add up to habits of faithfulness—those parts of your everyday life that you explicitly connect to your faith. Being clear and intentional will help the children around you see beyond your actions to the beliefs and scripture that are the foundation for your faithful actions.

I'll admit, I wasn't entirely clear on what all that meant. But I knew to be on the lookout for teaching moments; in fact I would be vigilant in doing so. That's because this spoke to something I have always believed about parenthood: if you want your child to do or be something, you must do or be that thing yourself. I'm not a "Do as I say, not as I do" person or parent. I knew early on Tain would more readily say "please" and "thank you" if he heard Darryl and me using those words often. The same would go for this journey. Tain would make his spiritual exploration and go with us as we made our own.

At the end of the tract was a prayer asking God for "calm strength and patient wisdom" so that we can teach our children to have "inquiring and discerning hearts, the courage to will and to persevere, a spirit to know and to love you, and the gift of joy and wonder in all your works."

I especially liked that "joy and wonder" part. It spoke of light, of the sense I felt was lacking at the first church I'd visited. Joy and wonder were gifts I wanted Tain to know were there—already there for him in abundance. I wasn't sure if that could be taught, so I didn't know how or if it would develop by coming to this old stone church and opening the red doors and walking through them every Sunday with Tain. But these were all things I wanted for him, and I already felt the faith and confidence that Trinity would be the place to begin.

Chapter 4

WHAT DOES GOD LOOK LIKE?

We have begun and begun badly. At the communion rail, I try to get Tain to dip his thin round white wafer into the wine, but he wants to chew on the morsel dry and then sip from the cup. "Okay," I whispered. A woman dressed in a black robe and a snowy linen top lowers the silver cup to his lips. Tain tastes it. He recoils. He doesn't spit it out—I'm relieved at that—but his face explodes with disgust and he rises from the kneeling cushion with his mouth open, his tongue hanging out. The woman who had offered the cup smiles gamely, and while I'm not embarrassed, I am glad we are seated in the far back left of the sanctuary: it is easy for Darryl to exit quietly with Tain so they can go to the bathroom and rinse his mouth to wash away the wine's sting. I can sympathize with him, though, because I've never liked the taste of alcohol. Only my adult reserve keeps me from reacting the same way Tain did when I sip the wine.

We started attending Trinity on January 2, 2011, thinking this would be a fine way to start the New Year. I guess I was thinking going to church might be a New Year's resolution people tried the same way they did with wanting to lose weight, perhaps inspired by the experience of going to a Christmas service over the holidays. This turned out to be a bit of a strange morning, before being capped off by Tain's awkward first communion. It was the day after a holiday so there was no Sunday school—or "church school" as it was called there. I also realized what we were thinking of as the beginning of the year was not really that, liturgically or curriculum-wise, for Trinity. Church school operated on the regular school calendar, so it had been in session since September. Tain would be starting mid-year. And I had yet to learn the liturgical calendar, so I didn't realize the new church year had begun several weeks earlier with Advent and at this point was homing in on Epiphany.

We took seats, as I said, near the rear, the better to observe everything. I perused the bulletin, which, the pastor noted at the start, contained all the words of the service. The bulletin was ten pages, at least, and I wondered how long it would take for every word to be read or recited. I recognized my old impatience with long services—visions of the decorated chairs at the front of the church for a Catholic wedding ceremony still in the back of my head. Tain fidgeted, and I tried to get him to follow along with the words in the bulletin. I used the small pencil I'd found in the book rack on the back of the pew and filled out the card for new visitors, and then gave the pencil to Tain so he could draw in the bulletin. I was grateful when an usher came over and offered him a children's storybook Bible; Tain said thank you and sat turning the pages while the pastor delivered her sermon. I recognized her as the same woman who'd spoken to Tain's preschool two years earlier.

She talked about the letter to the Ephesians, which I didn't know, though it sounded like a very good thing to read.

"Have we lived our faith as an adventure?" she asked. I liked the concept, but didn't know what it meant or how it appeared in practice. Looking back on this now, I see clearly that I didn't realize the adventure was just beginning. But I wrote down the question to ponder at another time. I also wrote: *Have I nourished my faith? How can I let go and be more open, more forgiving?*

The pastor mentioned thinking about what it would be like to see through the eyes of Christ. I could ponder this as well. I liked that the sermon felt like a thoughtful conversation, and I could listen to her without tension. I didn't feel that I had to hold onto myself, as I did when listening to a charismatic-type preacher (picture the actor Ian McKellan preaching in the film *Cold Comfort Farm*) warning about the wages of sin and death so forcefully that I felt as if my soul would be pulled out through the top of my head. And because I wasn't in that defensive mode, I could think about the questions and add my own: *What is in this place for me? What do I ask?*

After the communion catastrophe, Darryl and Tain returned before the end of the service in time to hear, "Go in peace to love and serve the Lord."

"Thanks be to God," the people responded.

Being at the back of the church put us near the front of the line to greet and speak to the pastor on our way out. We introduced ourselves and learned to call her Pastor Kathie. I let Tain know he could ask her questions and talk to her about God whenever he wanted to. She explained how next time he could go downstairs where the children have their own church service. He liked the sound of that. I remember he hugged her before we left the sanctuary.

A few days later we received a welcome letter from Pastor Kathie. "It is wonderful to have you here at Trinity and to worship with all of you." She acknowledged, "You may have journeyed to us by way of a far different tradition and find yourself confused or overwhelmed. We invite your questions and reflections." Somehow this was comforting—it didn't sound like this was a place of closed minds and closed doors. This was a place of invitation, of questions and reflection. And the way Tain had taken to Pastor Kathie felt encouraging. He has always had strong radar for picking up on people he likes. If he had felt uncomfortable in any way Tain would have said so. And the fact that he wasn't turned off by what happened at communion was a small victory.

Our next Sunday at Trinity the following week was quite different. Instead of having my eyes glued to the bulletin I could look around more and take in the theatrical aspect of the service—the choir decked out in black and white, processing down the aisle behind a tall boy in a hooded white robe carrying a large gold cross, Pastor Kathie bringing up the rear. Darryl said the service was very similar to a Catholic one, and I recalled the Episcopal connection to the Church of England and how England had been Catholic before Henry VIII started having marital issues. I appreciated the elegance of the process and the motion parishioners made when they crossed themselves—I'd only witnessed that in films before. Months later I would purchase a Trinity tee-shirt listing Robin Williams's "Top 10 Reasons to be an Episcopalian." My favorite reason is connected to this aspect of the service: "All of the pageantry—none of the guilt."

At the end of the opening procession, Pastor Kathie spoke a prayer, then there was more music as the robed boy came back down the aisle, this time holding before him a smaller gold cross. Children came tumbling out of the pews to follow it, heading down for the "children's liturgy" we'd heard of. Tain seemed primed for the adventure and followed them. I noticed I had no qualms about his going. I don't know if this was because the space was now familiar or because we had friends in the congregation and he knew a few of the children in the group.

▪▪▪▪ Tain's Take

When I started going to Trinity church, I was about six years old. I was very excited about going to church. Trinity is a big church. Well, it felt big to me because I was very little. I used to go to Trinity for preschool, so I knew where it was. The sanctuary is the biggest room in the church. It has a lot of pews and stained glass windows. The window that I liked the most was the one that had a big Jesus on it. They all were very colorful. The first time we went, when the service started I didn't really understand what was going on, or what Pastor Kathie was doing. But the next week, at the beginning of the service, someone walked down the aisle holding a golden cross. All of the children came out of their pews and followed it. My mom told me to follow the cross as well.

We went downstairs and into a little room. A woman was standing behind a small altar that had two unlit candles on it. "Good morning," she said. She looked at me and could tell that I was new. "I haven't seen you before, what is your name?" She asked me.

"Hi, my name is Tain," I said.

She told me that her name was Mrs. Vogelman. She said that before we started children's liturgy, we had to light the candles. Another girl and I lit them while Mrs. Vogelman helped us. After that, she played a piano and sang. Then she reached into a drawer and pulled out a purple box.

"This box is special. Does anyone know why?"

A little boy raised his hand and said, "Because it is the story box."

"That's right. Now I am going to open this box, and it will tell a story of Jesus."

When she opened the box, she pulled out some green, black, and blue fabric and put them neatly on the floor. She got out some little sheep figures, and a figure of a man.

"The shepherd takes care of the sheep. He takes them to get drinks."

She moved the sheep and the shepherd over to the blue fabric. "And he keeps them out of danger."

She moved the sheep to the edge of the black fabric, but used the shepherd to move them away. "And then, the shepherd takes the sheep back home when the day is done."

She moved the sheep back to the green part. "But if one of his hundred sheep goes missing, he will go out into the wild, to bring it back home, and leave the other ninety-nine," she said.

I thought it was very interesting that the shepherd would leave the other sheep to look for the one. She said, "In this story, Jesus was the shepherd, and we were the sheep."

I was confused who Jesus was and why we were sheep. But then the man with the cross came downstairs, and we all went back upstairs. Back upstairs at the service, we sang hymns and then we had communion. We all went up to the altar. There were long pillows along the rail with pictures of times when Jesus lived. We all kneeled on the pillows and Pastor Kathie came down and started to hand things out. The things that she passed out were little wafers that represented the bread that Jesus gave. When she gave it to us she said, "The body of Christ, the bread of Heaven."

I slowly ate the wafer. I thought that it tasted like cardboard. Then another lady came and held out a cup for us to sip. When she held it out to me she said, "The blood of Christ, the cup of salvation."

When we first came to church the week before I did not know what the drink was, so I tried it. Whatever the drink was, I did not like the awful taste. My dad took me to the bathroom to wash out the bad taste in my mouth. He told me that the drink that I didn't like was wine and that a lot of people don't like the taste. When we came back into the sanctuary, we were almost done singing the closing hymn. When we finished the song, Pastor Kathie said, "Go in peace! Alleluia!" And then everyone else said, "Thanks be to God! Alleluia!" And then it was time to leave.

I liked my first days at church. It was nice to experience it. I asked my mom who I could talk to so I could learn more about Jesus. She said that if I ever needed to talk to someone about what church was about, or what Jesus did, I could talk to Pastor Kathie. I did talk to Pastor Kathie a lot. She had black hair and round glasses. She usually wore a big robe and a yellow stole with pictures of children on it. One reason that I like her is that she knows how to talk to younger kids like me.

■ ■ ■ ■

When Tain returned with the other children during the Peace, he had a folded newsletter with a line drawing on the cover depicting the story from one of the readings from the service. I reminded him to shake hands and say the word "peace" to the people around us. He did this easily, and I remember how the adults smiled at him and seemed to enjoy Tain's outgoing nature. Then he sat down with his newsletter and continued to draw on it while I pondered Pastor Kathie's words from earlier in the service, this sermon about a girl who didn't think she was a sinner like those around her.

To my surprise Tain didn't hesitate to have another go at communion. Pastor Kathie pressed the wafer into his hands. "Tain, the body of Christ, the bread of heaven," she said. A woman, different from the previous week, followed with the wine and she offered it to Tain. "The blood of Christ, the cup of salvation," she said. This time Tain peered into the cup and, grasping the wafer carefully between his thumb and forefinger, dipped it into the wine so it absorbed just the tiniest bit of the liquid. Then he popped it into his mouth and smiled at me as he chewed, as if he'd been receiving communion his whole life. If it had been appropriate, I would have said to him, *You go, baby!*

After the service, we went to the hall where Tain had once attended preschool. The children's minister, Mrs. Vogelman, gave us a registration form to complete and showed us the room where Tain's age group would have their class. There were children already seated, and a woman with light brown hair was passing a snack of crackers and cups of water. Tain kissed me on the cheek. "Bye, Mama!"

"Okay, bud," I said. "See you in a bit. Be good. Listen to your teacher."

Darryl and I waited in the room called the undercroft, an all-purpose area where the preschool staged indoor recess during bad weather. There was coffee offered there, as well as donuts and bagels. There was a room divider at one end—here, I learned, was where they held children's liturgy. Right then in that area there seemed to be a church school class for older children that was about to start. Before the teacher closed the door, I noticed the children had a piano and their own small altar in the room, and on it was a large gold cross, flanked by candles. Darryl and I filled cups with coffee and tea and we spoke to a few people and tried to blend in. Actually, being low-key might be a better way to describe it. It's hard for me to blend in anywhere in our town because there are so few people of color, and the same went for that room. But I didn't feel uncomfortable on that score. It's just much harder being a stranger in a room where everyone else already knows each other. I could tell that for some sitting at the tables this was a weekly routine, and I wondered if fellowship time would ever feel that familiar to us. How long would it take for us to feel comfortable there?

An hour later children walked through the halls ringing bells—the signal that church school was over. I signed Tain out of his class and thanked the teacher and asked how Tain had been. On the drive home I asked him about what he had learned in church school, and he told me about the craft project they had made. Okay. That was not the answer I expected. I'm not sure what I expected. I didn't expect a theological treatise, but I thought he would at least mention a Bible story. I reminded myself this was just the beginning, and it was his journey, not mine.

Once we started attending church, I loved that Tain and I had a new language in which to converse. Tain could begin to put words and sometimes images to what he thought about God. I felt this was important, because it could help Tain recognize that the mysterious, loving presence he felt around him is real and can be relied upon. So I continued to ask about church school. I didn't want to drop any balls; I wanted to be on top of things, looking for those teaching moments—as the tract had described. I wanted, at least, to expand upon any concepts he found difficult.

On the way home from Sunday worship, less than a month after that first church school class, I asked Tain what he and his friends had discussed in church school.

"We talked about faith," he said.

"Okay," I said. "That's a tough one. Faith is when you believe in something even though you can't see it. Like with God. Do you understand that? It's about having faith in God who you can't see."

"But Mama, I see God everywhere. I even see him at the post office!"

My head spun around and I looked at him settling himself into the backseat and fastening his seatbelt. I was stunned speechless. I didn't know how to respond, and yet I knew not to challenge Tain's words. His certainty was shattering, as if it would reduce a wall of disbelief to rubble—this little Joshua, my opaque wall of Jericho. My fingers trembled a bit as I oriented the car keys in my hand and aimed for the ignition switch. "Okay!" I said, and I nodded. "You're right!"

I posted this story on my Facebook feed and wrote, "The kid is right! And I'll be on my best behavior at the post office from now on. . . ." I was being tongue-in-cheek, but what Tain said did make me open my eyes and think anew. Was I looking for God anywhere and everywhere? Had I forgotten how to seek and see through my own childlike eyes? I began to sense how deep this pool was in which we were swimming. I'm a poor swimmer in real life—I can't even tread water. I began to feel the same kind of inadequacy here. In the weeks and months to come, I would utter some version of these words—*"You're right, Tain! Okay! That's great! All right! Yes."*—again and again, and at times when I would least expect to do so. I had to get used to being prepared, in those "teaching moments," whenever I think I'm going to teach Tain something, for a very different result: he could, and usually did, end up teaching me about faith.

On another day, he comes from class with a picture he's drawn. He tells me they were asked to draw a picture of God. I am surprised and fascinated by how Tain seems to have had no trouble doing so. In Tain's vision, God has big googly eyes, long golden jewelry hanging from large ears and rows of rings on outstretched fingers. I love how Tain seems to be seeing God as larger than life, with ears big enough to listen to all prayers and a broad reach seeking to embrace everyone. I tape the picture to the door in our family room and there it stays for months. At some point I carefully remove it and put it away in a box of Tain's keepsakes. I keep the picture, because if I forget what God looks like I want to be able to remember.

Another of Tain's interesting thoughts: In the car one afternoon on the way home from school, I heard Tain singing a VeggieTales song, the one about how God is bigger than the bogeyman. "Tain, what is a bogeyman?" I asked.

"He's a man who boogies and plays the saxophone. Why else would they call him the boogieman?"

The journalist in me knows I should have asked a follow-up question: "Why does it matter whether or not God is bigger than a guy playing a saxophone?" But I was smiling. If Tain can make something that is supposed to be scary into a dancing musician, I say more power to him. *"You're right, Tain! Okay! That's great! All right! Yes."*

As I said, I felt out of my depth, but why should that matter? As long as Tain was in there swimming laps around me like an Olympian, wasn't that what was important? Wasn't this about developing his faith, and wasn't I already a believer? Did I need something in this too? Initially I thought this feeling had something to do with being dissatisfied with my work: my business as an editor and ghostwriter had overrun my creative writing life, and I was trying to find my way back to being a novelist again. But my reactions to our early experience at Trinity told me I was hungering for something else. I didn't know what it was or even how to begin to feed it.

Goethe says when you make a move, Providence moves with you. Help shows up, and you receive the assistance you never knew you needed. About two weeks after we started attending Trinity, the author and speaker Matthew Kelly came to town. One of the programs he teaches, "Living Every Day with Passion and Purpose," is based on his book *The Rhythm of Life*. At the time I was part of a group of five goal-oriented women seeking to adjust our life compasses. One of the women, my friend Joanne, had seen the DVD version of the program in a class at her church, St. Rose of Lima, and brought it to our group. Matthew is Catholic and aware of the need to re-energize the faith. In fact, his organization is called the Dynamic Catholic Institute. (Tag line: *Be Bold. Be Catholic.*) But his messages have had great appeal with secular audiences, including the one encouraging people to become the best versions of themselves; in my group we were seeking to do exactly that. Matthew was born in Sydney, Australia, so of course we loved his accent, but also his humor and confidence. I liked his combination of authority and vulnerability—he talked a lot about his love of chocolate to the detriment of his waistline, and I found his acknowledged helplessness in the face of such a love particularly endearing.

That January, Joanne scored a coup bringing Matthew to St. Rose for a sold-out event. I got up early that Saturday morning so my friends and I would have front-row seats. I took away something from his talk that has left a mark on my journey. Matthew talked about going to church in the morning, running through the things he had to do that day, and taking particular note of what God could help him with, if he was willing. But, he said, things didn't really change until he added one more thing, a very important element: listening for what God might be saying to him.

He showed us this clever little pocket-sized book he'd created, a "Mass Journal," designed so you could be in a mindset of active discernment at church and write down what you were hearing as you listened to the sermon and participated in worship. What you wrote, ideally, would become the focus of your actions, thoughts, and prayers for the coming week. As Matthew described this and I was already deciding to take such a notebook with me next time I went to church, he presented us with a surprise: we would each get a Mass Journal to take home. It's almost ridiculous how thrilled I was to receive that little blue book, especially when any old spiral-bound notebook would have been fine. But I felt it was the best gift, the right gift, to receive at that moment. It gave me the means of making a shift in focus I didn't know I needed. I went from thinking about what was going on with Tain as I sat in the pew week to week, to paying attention to my own faith.

What is faith? I thought either you had it or you didn't. If I had it, why exactly sit there in church? But if I feel God is close and personal to me, then isn't that like having a friend? And shouldn't I cultivate and nurture that relationship as I would with any friend? As *The Little Prince* says, to have a friend takes time. Developing a relationship with God takes time. Matthew was offering me another way to be in relationship with God. What he wrote in his Mass Journal, he said, was a starting point for his conversation with God in prayer. He suggested praying, "God, show me one way in this Mass I can become a better version of myself this week!"

The next time I went to Trinity I took my little blue book with me. I placed it on the pew beside me with a pen on top of it and I waited. I listened. I eventually wrote, *"Time, talent, and treasure. How can I share my time and talent in a way that will make me a better version of myself?"* I didn't come up with an answer that day, only another question. And I wondered if this is how it would be—that this journey with Tain would be a path of question marks. But I continued keeping the "Mass Journal." Rather quickly the entries lengthened—not too long, because there was only enough space for one square set of lines per entry. They were long enough, though, for me to feel encouraged:

> *January 30, 2011: Have compassion for others AND myself. Think in terms of community. I am not alone.*
>
> *February 6, 2011: Live in a way that would not make sense to others if God did not exist. Be the mystery. Live simply in faith. Be alive on every level. Be spiritual. SHINE in the spirit! Experience the super-aliveness that comes from Grace. Feel the warmth of my own heart.*
>
> *February 13, 2011: How can I be more kind so that my first thought and feeling is kindness? Forgiveness is the first step. "Make holy that which is common." Remember the call to love.*

February 20, 2011: Again, forgiveness. How can I be more forgiving, more kind? AGAPE: unconditional love. The love that takes all our strength and energy. We must WILL it into being. Love even those I think I cannot. Look into every face and see my sister or brother. Love the world as God loves us.

The entries continue for many consecutive Sundays, because we went to church every week. This was a considerable feat when you consider that just as we started attending Trinity, it snowed week after week in depths of historic proportions. During one storm in late January the snow fell in parts of Connecticut at a rate of nearly four inches an hour. The plows pushed aside the drifts into walls that grew to nearly five feet high. Darryl and I had to shovel a tunnel path from our driveway, up the back steps and across our deck, so the oil deliveryman could pull his hose there to fill our tank. In other homes, oil tanks ran dry because the owners couldn't move the snow themselves and anyone they could have paid to do it was already too busy. Some plow drivers broke their equipment in the heavy snow and found themselves stranded as well. Ancient barns collapsed all over the countryside from the weight of the snow, and homeowners feared the same fate for their houses.

And still we rose on Sunday mornings, pulled on boots, hooded sweatshirts, and heavy sweaters, and made our way to church.

At the end of our first month Tain returned from children's liturgy holding a large cloth doll that had long, dark brown yarn hair and a beard. It was dressed in a white shift with a red robe over it. "Whatcha got there?" Darryl asked Tain.

"It's Jesus!" he replied, his delight spilling over. Tain handed me a cloth bag that went with the doll. Inside was a children's book entitled *If Jesus Came to My House*, and a binder. The binder contained an explanation that the Jesus Doll was a special ministry at Trinity. Each week a child could take the doll home, read the book, and report back with thoughts and images relating to what they learned from having Jesus with them at their house. The binder contained the pages from Jesus's previous trips home with Trinity children.

"Oh my goodness, Tain, that's cool!" I said, and I meant it. I thought the whole concept was absolutely brilliant. Why shouldn't a child have a physical depiction to help them focus on Christ and his lessons? The book depicts Jesus as another child; a little boy in the book thinks about all the help and hospitality he would offer if Jesus were to visit the little boy's home: the best seat, his favorite toy. Tain hugged Jesus and even took him to the rail with him when it was time for communion.

Throughout the week, I was surprised by how well Tain looked after the doll. We took lots of pictures: There was Jesus sitting next to Tain while Tain played on the computer. There were Tain and Jesus sitting in our meditation room, wrapped in a blanket. There were Tain and Jesus sitting in the tent Tain had set up in his bedroom, and there was Tain sleeping with Jesus in his bed.

Here are some of Tain's notes that I typed up for him for the binder, dated January 30–February 5, 2011:

Jesus got a tour of my house.
I was so happy he was at my house.
He got to do everything with me.
He told me he knew about dinosaurs.
He taught me to be nice to guys who come to my house.
I liked that he teaches me things.

What's not mentioned in these notes or in my Mass Journal is the conversation Darryl and I had been having with Tain's pediatrician and ear-nose-throat specialist. For months, Tain had been tolerating ear infections. From Darryl he had inherited large adenoids that prevented his nose and ears from draining properly. We kept going through cycles of Tain's experiencing ear pain and the doctor prescribing antibiotics, which always worked—but then Tain would soon develop another infection. We had been waiting to see if Tain would outgrow the problem before proceeding with a surgical alternative, but that February, after a terrible six-week period of ongoing infections and antibiotics, we decided with the specialist that it was time for him to have his tonsils and adenoids removed and temporary ear tubes put in place to help with the drainage.

When Tain took the Jesus Doll back after his week was up, I found Mrs. Vogelman after church and asked if it might be possible to have the doll again in a few days' time. I told her about Tain's upcoming surgery and how he'd never been in the hospital before or had such a medical procedure done. I thought it might be a good idea to have Jesus with him. She said it was fine—in fact there are two Jesus dolls for this very reason, so that both could be in rotation as needed and the children wouldn't have to wait long to take Jesus home. She gave Tain the Jesus doll he'd returned, and he was thrilled.

A picture we took for the Jesus binder shows Tain holding and leaning against Jesus, a look of question and concern on his face. There's another of him sitting in a wheelchair holding the doll while a nurse buttons up Tain's coat. Tain wrote:

I was a little bit scared. When I went in for the surgery Jesus came with me. I was scared because they put something over my mouth. It smelled bad and I fell asleep.

They brought me back to my room. I woke up. I didn't feel good. It felt like there was stuff in my mouth. But Jesus was there. He was wearing my socks! And indeed, in the picture there is Jesus, on the shelf next to Tain's bed. Tain is asleep.

Jesus was helping me the whole time.

When I look back on that time I know Jesus was helping me too. Because after the surgery I had to figure out how to handle Tain's suffering. He had the usual post-operative pain and discomfort. He seemed bewildered by how much his throat hurt, and he cried in that frustrated way a child cries when he has been woken before he has finished sleeping. I knew he was in pain, but there was something else about him that troubled me: I sensed a sadness about him, almost a depression. It was as though he had been sucked down into a sinkhole and, if allowed, would stay down there, crying and contemplating the darkness.

I wanted to do something, but it wasn't a matter of wanting to ease his pain or get him painkillers or anything like that. I'm not sure how to explain this; I felt the need to honor his pain. I think that was my instinct.

When I was in college I'd seen a TV movie called *Alex: The Life of a Child* based on the book by sportswriter Frank Deford. It's the story of the brief life of his daughter who died at the age of eight from cystic fibrosis. There's a scene where Alex, during one of the many hospital visits she experienced, is having trouble breathing and tells the doctor on call that her lung has collapsed. She knows because this has happened before and she knows what the pain feels like. The doctor tells her she's wrong and leaves. Another caregiver eventually helps Alex, and in the morning her father, who now knows what happened, overhears a nurse telling the doctor that Alex was right—she did have a collapsed lung. The doctor says something to the effect of, "Oh well, no harm done." Mr. Deford takes him to task with words that have stayed with me ever since. He said there was harm done because his daughter, who lives in pain, has now been led to believe her doctors have no faith in her pain.

I am in tears even now as I recall the phrase—*faith in her pain.* I can't tell you what that means, but I do know it was in my heart when I began to act on his behalf that afternoon after his surgery. I wanted him to know that I and everyone else who loved him had faith in his pain. We wouldn't deny it or ignore or try to humor him into doing the same. We would be in it with him and help him as much as we could. While Darryl sat with him, I went outside and called our friends, the Trottas, to see if their daughter Thea could come over that afternoon. Thea and Tain were four and in the same preschool class at Trinity when I first met Maria and her husband, Gian, at an autumn fair held at a local farm. Tain and Thea did everything together that day: petting cows, naming rabbits, riding ponies, getting pulled around in a hay cart. Maria, Gian, and I (Darryl wasn't with me that day) discovered we had a lot in common: both families had recently moved from New York City. Gian used to work at Time Inc., as did I. Each had an only child.

I have never seen two children take to each other the way Tain and Thea did. They maintained this affection and closeness even when they didn't go to school together for several years. People often think they are siblings. The fact that they argue, play, and love like siblings adds to the illusion. When they were very young and walking down the street, as when trick-or-treating, I enjoyed how they would hold hands, unbidden. The Trottas quickly became our family here. We spent holidays together, sharing the Newtown Labor Day Parade and meeting up in Central Park for the Macy's Thanksgiving Day Parade.

Sometimes on a Saturday, Gian or Maria or both of them together would take the kids to the aquarium or a museum. Tain and Thea used to play soccer, and during their practices, Gian and I would sit in the field in folding chairs and talk and laugh all morning. He would tell me about when he was a sports correspondent in Italy covering the great soccer teams of the world. Maria and I had this idea of one day taking a house in Italy for eight weeks over the summer so Tain and Thea could play with kids there and maybe pick up the language. I was so grateful and full of joy to have such friends who were like family to us.

So Thea came over, and though Tain couldn't talk to her much, she fussed over him in a way that I'm sure was more fun and more acceptable to him than if I were doing it.

This all happened on a Thursday. The doctor said Tain should return for a post-op examination the following Friday and expect to be out of school for a week. But again acting on my instinct, I contacted Ms. Coppola, Tain's teacher. Tain may be an only child, but he is social, and something told me his recovery would be better if he could have the company of his friends and enjoy their activity and laughter. At home, he would most likely stay on the couch, watch television, and grow sullen. So, I told Ms. Coppola I wanted to try sending Tain to school that Monday. I explained what he could and couldn't eat. I spoke to the school nurse as well and informed her of what we were doing and what Tain could have for pain medication if he needed any. Granted, if he were going to the school he attends now, a large, bustling public school, I would not have considered this. But at this time, he was in a private school, just eight to ten children in his first-grade class, and plenty of watchful adult eyes around.

From the moment Tain returned, his classmates hugged and applauded him as though he were an astronaut back from the moon. They knew of his surgery, an adventure none of them had ever experienced, so they were happy to have one of their own back to tell the tale. The children cared for him too— if they were having snack and one of them noticed only one yogurt left, he or she would grab it for Tain—they all knew he needed to eat soft food—a demonstration of the people around him having faith in his pain. Tain absorbed all the affection of his classmates and picked up the rhythm of school again. For my part I made sure that each night he got plenty of sleep, and in the mornings he dressed warmly enough so he could play outside for recess.

At the end of the week I took Tain to his follow-up appointment, as scheduled, and the doctor marveled at how well he looked. His ears and throat were healing well and Tain was cheerful and glowing.

"He's doing really well. I don't think I've ever seen a child recover this fast from surgery. What did you do?"

I smiled. "I sent him to school."

Tain has about ten pages in the Jesus binder representing at least ten weeks Jesus spent at our house. I admit, there did come a point where Tain would show up with the Jesus doll and Darryl and I would sigh heavily and maybe even roll our eyes. It was an added task to our busy lives—we had to remember to take pictures with the doll, then remind Tain he had to think about what he wanted to write for the binder, then get him to sit down at the kitchen computer and get it done. I wondered if he would eventually have nothing to write. What else did Tain have to learn from Jesus? But it turned out to be a lot. What I learned and what impressed me most is how many times in the later pages Tain is photographed with his friends and Jesus. No one seemed to mind, no one questioned this or teased him. Some of his entries:

> *Jesus came to my house and my friend K's house . . . Jesus helped K when he was having trouble sharing.*
>
> *My papa and I played with Jesus and my new friend "C.J." I found C.J. at a tag sale. Jesus taught me that I can't always get what I want. And he taught me I need to pay my mom back when she buys something for me when I don't have my wallet.*
>
> *Jesus came to Maundy Thursday service with me. At that service I got my feet washed and I washed someone else's feet, just like Jesus did. I sang at the Good Friday service and we talked about Jesus. I was glad to have Jesus with me for Easter.*

Tain's friends seemed just as glad to have Jesus around. And, in fact, so was I. There came a point when I considered buying

Tain a Jesus doll of his own. But Jesus isn't cheap—this particular doll cost nearly $100. It's not even made anymore. The liturgical shop in Ohio that once sold those dolls closed. I do appreciate the connection the doll fostered in Tain. I'd even say it's priceless.

■■■■ Tain's Take

When I used to go to children's liturgy at church, we had something we called the Jesus doll. Every week one of us would take Jesus home and bring him back the week after. The Jesus doll was very important to me because it made me feel like he would actually come to my house and visit. I did a lot of things with Jesus, like going to my friends' houses, bringing him to dinner, and even bringing him to the store. But I think that the time I took home Jesus that was most important to me was when I took Jesus to the hospital with me.

I had to get my tonsils taken out, and I took Jesus. When I went in, I was afraid, but I knew that I had Jesus with me. We played with the toys in the waiting room, and sat in the hospital bed. They put a plastic mask over my face and I fell asleep. When I woke up, I had Jesus there with me. We were then taken to another room in a wheelchair. Jesus was helping me get through this the whole time! This showed that I had a great connection with Jesus. I felt like Jesus was one of my friends. And that made me feel good. He made me feel happy when I was sad, he was with me when I needed someone. I really loved Jesus because he liked to help people, just like I do. He also helped me know to be nice to others. I was probably the kid in children's liturgy who took Jesus home the most. Sometimes, I felt like I wasn't sharing Jesus enough. But I always wanted to take him home because he was very special to me. But the other kids took home Jesus as well.

■ ■ ■ ■

On Community

About a year or so ago I was in New York City with Tain and we found ourselves near Saint Patrick's Cathedral. I explained to him that it was a very big, very famous church and that Papa had once taken his mother there for Christmas Eve service when she was visiting us from Ohio. We went inside, and Tain was awed by the cavernous height of the place and the number of people milling about and praying in the pews.

"I could never go to church here," he whispered to me.

"Oh? How come?"

"I could never remember everyone's name."

I laughed because this made me recall a time not long after we started attending Trinity when Tain and I were in the community room known as the undercroft. Rick, an older man with black, gray-flecked hair, who had been one of the first people who greeted us early on, smiled at us and said hello to me and then to Tain: "Hey, little buddy, how are you?"

Tain, with his usual straightforward candor responded. "Who are you?"

I was about to chime in with "Tain, you remember, this is Mr. Rick" but Rick answered before I could speak. He said, "I'm someone who is a part of this community and who would keep an eye out for you if your parents aren't around."

The clarity and truth of his answer surprised me, because here was an aspect of coming to Trinity that I hadn't considered. In bringing Tain to church, we were also giving him community. It was a gift I hadn't expected—here was a community, a place where Tain would encounter and know adults of all ages and they would know him. I was surprised this didn't factor more into my thinking about church, because usually, since Tain is an only child and we live far from where Darryl and I grew up, I think a lot about what people he has around him. On the long, hilly street where we live we are close enough to know some of our neighbors, but once the weather gets cold we rarely see each other. Still, Tain knows their names, and for his third and fourth birthdays he invited our next-door neighbors and their eighth- and ninth-grade teenagers, and their cat as well. (The cat demurred but everyone else attended.)

When I was a kid not only did we know our neighbors, but I had cousins and an uncle and aunt (my father's sister) living next door. Daddy also made a point at regular intervals of loading all of us kids up in the station wagon and driving us to the next town over to visit our maternal grandfather and my mother's sisters and their children—our host of cousins. We do make a trip at least once a year to visit our families and Tain's young cousins, but I knew he wouldn't have such an experience very often. And being at home in the world means being connected to other people and knowing how to nurture those connections.

Now here was Tain in a faith community, getting connected with people who can model belief and affirm his faith. He is surrounded by people, young and old, doing the same activities— singing hymns, reciting psalms, consuming the bread and wine of communion, praying—who all profess and praise the presence of the living God. What Rick said to Tain was an encouragement for me as well to make sure we got ourselves to Trinity each week. If we only went once a month or every six weeks we would have to relearn details such as names and start again to find our way in this new world. I would reinforce the names. "Hey Tain, there's Rick. There's Martha. There's Larry. Go say hello."

Since then, I've noticed that the experiences and activities Tain likes and thrives in the best are the ones where he has a strong sense of community. He is a Boy Scout; he acts both in Drama Club at his school and in a theatre program called NewArts; he regularly attends events at Camp Washington, the retreat center run by the Episcopal Church in Connecticut; and he is in the Trinity

Choristers, our church's children's choir. Another mom recently said to me, "Tain does so much! You always have him in a lot of things." But I don't think of it as having him in a bunch of activities. It's all about community. I also don't believe in overscheduling, so I'm cautious with how things fall in Tain's calendar. The activities he continues to do (he has dropped sports and groups along the way) are the ones he not only enjoys, but where he feels a deep connection, even a commitment to everyone, children and adults, involved in the activity or organization. "We're like a family," he once said of his NewArts friends.

The choristers, I think, were the ones who helped give Tain his initial grounding at Trinity. Early on at the worship services, he had noticed the children swathed in black and white, with a few dressed in black only, processing two by two down the aisle behind the large gold cross. "Those kids are in the choir," I told him. "Do you think you'd like to do that?"

He nodded.

"Okay, I'll look into it. I'll ask."

I loved the idea because I was already thinking that having Tain sit quietly in the pew with his parents would only last so long. The service—even though going to children's liturgy meant he didn't have to sit through most of it—was long and boring for a six-year-old. One Sunday he fidgeted so much in the pew while waiting for the post-communion prayer that he slipped off the kneeler and bumped his chin on the pew in front of him. If he were with the choristers at least he would have a role and, I hoped, would have another way to own the whole church experience.

As it turned out, Tain was a year too young for the choristers. First he had to join the primary choir, which featured children in first grade and younger. The small group sang in high-pitched angelic voices of how "Jesus's hands were kind hands," and, on

Easter morning, "the angels rolled the stone away." There was even a large papier mâché boulder that Tain helped the bigger kids roll up and down the aisle to the delight of everyone in the pews.

In fall, Tain donned the plain black robe of a novice chorister. He had to earn this privilege by spending a few services studying the bulletin and filling out a worksheet for Mrs. Sutherland, the music minister and organist, that showed he knew when the hymns, psalms, and offertory anthem occurred. The choristers rehearsed on Tuesday and Thursday afternoons; Tain only had to attend one rehearsal a week, but I took him both days. We had the time, and I thought it would be good for him so he could get up to speed—and by that I mean jelling with the other choristers. He'd taken piano lessons for over a year at that point, so I wasn't worried about the musical part. Besides, Tain has his father's ear. He can pick up notes, hearing pitches with good accuracy. Still, it struck me when sitting in the church library while the choristers practiced across the hall in the choir room that I could pick out Tain's voice. He sounded so strong and clear.

The choristers studied music theory in Voice for Life, a choral training curriculum offered through the Royal School of Church Music, and earned colored ribbons they wore around their necks as symbols of their accomplishments. Tain was proud to have a folder of sheet music with his name on it, and his own hymnal. Mrs. Sutherland expected a lot of the children, and I appreciated the way she challenged them. She wanted them to be on time, or rather, early, for their rehearsals and performances. She quizzed them throughout rehearsal. "What does 'presto' mean?" "Where's the eighth note in this measure?" They prayed at the start and end of each practice.

It was a wonderful shift, a new focus. Even better, Tain had discovered his own community within the larger Trinity community, because the choristers operated as a kind of family. The older kids, aged fourteen or so, shepherded the younger ones. Like watchful big brothers and sisters, they escorted them from church school—they had to leave early to get ready for the service—helped them get into their robes, and made sure they had their music and were lined up properly for the procession. It was impressive to see them all come down together from the choir loft and take up the whole of the communion rail. During the Peace, Tain liked to come down from the choir loft to find us, then work his way back, shaking hands and declaring, "Peace!"

I don't want you to think Tain's experience in the choristers was always an enthusiastic one. Like any kid, he had his days where he didn't want to go to rehearsal or got shushed for making too much noise in the choir loft during Pastor Kathie's sermon. He also valued going to children's liturgy, so the first couple of years he was in choir we had to figure out how to balance the two so he wouldn't miss out on either. But I could see how proud he was in the fall of 2012 when he was "whited," earning the snowy cotta he now wears over his black robe. He's grinning and giving two thumbs up in the photo I took. The same went for his first Voice for Life ribbon.

I like how, whether Tain knew it or not, the sounds of sacred music were being imprinted on his mind and in his being, music he would no doubt remember for the rest of his life. There were times at home when he would be playing quietly by himself and I'd hear him singing "Corpus Christi Carol." I listened and smiled, thinking how we'd come so far from "The Hairbrush Song" and "God Is Bigger Than the Bogeyman."

Chapter 5

OF HABITS AND RITUALS

When we first started at Trinity I thought about how the structure and routine of the Episcopal mass would be good for Tain. Seeing the same service over and over would give him a chance to become familiar with it and eventually better understand it. But the experience and practice of participating in prayerful activities again and again had many more levels of value than I had appreciated—these repetitions were incorporated into my life. I was writing in my Mass Journal every week; that was my own little ritual—quite personal and insular. But a ritual can have more powerful effects when the actions are physical, the words are spoken out loud, and the timeframe is spread out over the course of a year or even three. Matthew Kelly says our lives change when our habits change, and I was beginning to see the truth of his words. When I heard Tain singing his choir music to himself—in little ways like this he was changing, and so was I. And I found the large-scale structure of our church encouraged me to seek out personal ritual as well.

What I'm calling the large-scale structure is really the liturgical calendar. And I will admit I didn't know anything about it until Tain brought a picture of it from children's liturgy—a ring with different colors for each section. I found my own copy of this image and colored it in with my own crayons.

Advent (Royal Blue or Purple) The first season of the church year begins with the fourth Sunday before Christmas and continues through the day before Christmas. Advent means "coming," and it's a time of contemplation of and preparation for the birth of Christ.

Christmas (White or Gold) I'm still getting used to the idea that the Christmas season lasts twelve days, from Christmas Day until January 5, the day before Epiphany. At Trinity, the children are still adding to the crèche, depicting the arrival of the Three Kings days after Christmas, not on Christmas Eve.

Epiphany (White) This day represents the realization or manifestation of Christ's divinity. We celebrate the Baptism of our Lord on the First Sunday after Epiphany, and we often have baptisms at the church on that day.

Lent (Purple) This is the season of forty days extending from Ash Wednesday through Holy Saturday, not counting Sundays. (Sundays are considered feast days, but I'm still learning about feast days in the calendar. There are many other feast days outside of Lent.) The services on the last three days of Lent (Maundy Thursday, Good Friday, and Holy Saturday) are considered one long service without dismissal, the sacred Triduum. The *Book of Common Prayer* describes the Lenten season as marked by "self-examination and repentance; by prayer, fasting, and self-denial; and by reading and meditating on God's holy Word."

Easter (White) This is the big day, the most important of the faith, celebrating the resurrection of Christ on the third day after his crucifixion. The Easter season lasts fifty days—and again I have to remind myself of this because the secular world is quite focused on one-day holidays.

Pentecost (Red) Pentecost commemorates the descent of the Holy Spirit upon the apostles, fifty days after the resurrection of Christ. At Trinity, we decorate the church with red and white balloons, and the children return from children's liturgy wearing paper crowns with big orange and red flames.

Ordinary Time (Green) The two periods of ordinary time span the Monday after the Feast of the Baptism of our Lord through the Tuesday before Ash Wednesday, and the Monday after Pentecost through the Saturday before the First Sunday of Advent. Ordinary time makes me think of summer because of the color green and because the bulk of it happens then.

Starting to attend church in January as we did meant we only had about six weeks to settle in before Ash Wednesday and the start of Lent was upon us. The only thing I knew about Lent was that it happened every spring and my college friend Eileen would stop eating chocolate until it was over. If you add to this my focus on Tain's recovery from surgery on top of the harsh winter we were enduring, I'm sure no one would have blamed us if we had decided to let slide this first observation of Lent with the promise of picking it up the following year. But it felt as though we were already in the flow of Trinity events, so we didn't decide anything—we just rode the current.

Tain had the upper hand. "Wow, Tain, look at all the pretty purple!" I said, pointing out the new colors decorating the sanctuary.

"Yeah, Mama. It's for Lent. Didn't you know that?"

"Oh." Which meant no. Tain had already learned the key details about Lent in children's liturgy and church school. The little newsletter and coloring sheets he brought back taught me why the altar cloths and Pastor Kathie's garb were suddenly a striking shade of purple.

So, what would these next forty days be about besides not eating chocolate? I believed if I just kept showing up and doing what the other parishioners did, I'd figure it out somehow.

Pastor Kathie's sermons helped, and now that I think about it, I'm probably not the only person trying to figure out Lent every year. That's what our clergy is there for, to provide guidance. Pastor Kathie talked about how most people think they have to give up something for Lent, but instead they can take on something, such as a spiritual practice. The focus is the same: what can bring you closer to God? Viewed this way, giving up chocolate is not really an effective Lenten practice unless something about the way you consume it separates you from God. This made sense to me. *See the light and do not be afraid,* I wrote in my Mass Journal. *How do I live more in the light day by day? Know the signs by heart. Connect to him every day.*

I wrote in my Mass Journal, with a star next to it: *Give up TV for Lent.*

Why would I choose to give up television? At the time, television was a kind of companion for me, a way to keep voices in the house when I sat in my office working alone. I liked shows such as *The West Wing* that reminded me of the smart people I knew in college, and reality shows where people actually created things such as *Project Runway* and *Top Chef.* But what would it sound like if I sat in the quiet all day? What would I hear then?

On his own Tain also decided to give up television for Lent, but his choice was more specific: he would not watch his favorite cartoon, *Jake and the Neverland Pirates.* I didn't argue with this decision or ask him to come up with something more substantial or spiritual. The fact that he was thinking about it at all impressed me, and I let him go with it. Eventually I learned he was not just thinking about it, he was talking about it at school. More on that later.

For Ash Wednesday, our church had three services scheduled, morning, noon, and evening. I planned to take Tain to the early service in hopes that I could still get him to school on time by 8 A.M. Back then he attended a private school about a twenty-minute drive from our house. I'd seen mention of morning Ash Wednesday rituals on the local news and thought it seemed like a simple affair: you pray, the priest smears ashes on your forehead, then you leave and go about the day with the ashes marking you for the world to see. Some clergy even station themselves at coffee shops and train stations so the faithful can get "Ashes to Go" on their way to work. I figured it would be the same in-and-out process at Trinity.

Tain and I walked in, accepted the program from the usher with a smile, and sat in a pew near the front. I opened the program and quietly uttered, "What?" There it was, an entire prayer service, including Eucharist (communion). No quick anything. *This is going to take forever!* I thought. *He's going to be late for school.* I sat there hoping—and seriously I did this—that we would simply move through the service really fast, that they did that for the morning service because people had to go to work. Because I was so preoccupied with getting through the service, I wasn't absorbing the readings or the psalms. Tain, holding the Jesus doll, didn't seem concerned or impatient, so I tried to let go of my worry about traffic and our drive to school.

When it was time for the imposition of the ashes we went forward and knelt. Pastor Kathie, her finger dipped in oil and ashes, marked what I thought was a rather poetic-looking cross on Tain's forehead and said the words, "Remember that you are dust, and to dust you will return." She did the same for me, and we returned to our seat in the pew.

"Mama, what does that mean?" Tain whispered.

"What?"

"That we're dust and we'll return to dust."

"Shh," I whispered because the service was still going on. "We'll talk to Pastor Kathie about it on the way out."

But as I waited for the service to end I no longer was thinking about the time. Or I guess I was thinking about it in a different way. I thought of Hamlet in one of his soliloquies saying, "What is this quintessence of dust?" I thought of the miracle of our lives and what it means to be here in this time, in this moment. How would I explain this to Tain?

When the service ended and we gathered our things I told him, "It's a reminder. We come from the earth like all living things God made."

"But I don't want to be just dust," Tain said. And I knew that by this he meant, *I don't want to die.*

"Tain, you have a long time before you have to think about that. But you're here now. We're here now. It's about living your life and doing good things with this gift we have from God."

On our way out, we stopped to say goodbye to Pastor Kathie, and another parishioner caught my attention for a brief conversation. I noticed Tain talking to Kathie, and she seemed to be explaining something.

In the car, I wondered if what I had told him was too much. I glanced at him in the rearview mirror; he was just hugging the Jesus doll and looking out the window. His large brown eyes took it all in, and I knew he was continuing to ponder. There are photos in the Jesus doll binder where you can see the shadow of the small smudge of ashes on Tain's forehead. He wrote:

I went to Ash Wednesday service with Jesus. I still have a lot of questions about it. I wanted to know:

Why did I get ashes on my forehead?

Will we really turn into dust? Will it happen soon?

Is it true a part of us stays alive when we die? What part?

I remember reading this after I printed it out for Tain and thinking to myself, *I don't know either, Tain. I don't know.*

As a writer, I know it's important to be able to rest in and accept the place of not knowing. The poet John Keats called it negative capability. To be in such a space, for me anyway, requires a constant letting go and reminding myself it's okay not to know. How can a child come to learn this when they are in a period of nonstop questioning and learning and wanting to know? How will it be okay for Tain?

The harsh and historic winter of early 2011 had one more surprise for the Northeast: it didn't stick around. Everyone was expecting such a winter to wallop us with a late March or April snowstorm, but none developed. The days grew brighter on cue, and the bite in the air lessened as February wore on. Sure enough, when the time came, winter let go of us and ushered in a fabulous spring. The spring blossoms seemed particularly eager and bright that year. Even the hydrangea in my yard that hadn't bloomed since I planted it there from a pot five years previously produced a wealth of blue flowers. The trees blossomed heartily, and I recall the crabapple trees on the Trinity campus scented the whole parking lot with their intoxicating smell. Perhaps it was our reward for enduring the harsh winter.

Soon copies of trifold brochures with HOLY WEEK printed on the front appeared in the pews and on tables at the church entrances. It described a whole week of services beginning with Palm Sunday and culminating with Easter:

- Palm Sunday
- Monday: Taizé Service
- Tuesday: Morning Prayer
- Wednesday: Tenebrae
- Thursday: Maundy Thursday with foot washing (Afterward there would be something called the Watch, and there was a sign-up for time slots to sit in the chapel throughout the night keeping company with the Blessed Sacrament.)

- Friday: Good Friday
- Saturday: The Great Easter Vigil
- Easter Sunday

The brochure went on to describe the powerful experience of attending all the services, essentially accompanying Christ on his journey toward crucifixion and resurrection. The idea captured my imagination and I began to wonder: what would happen if I went to church every day that week? I would have to try this adventure without Tain. He would be in school for Tuesday's morning prayer, and all the evening services during the week started just when he was supposed to be in bed. The Tenebrae service, I noticed, didn't seem particularly kid-friendly. It ended in complete darkness marked by a thunderclap sound representing the earthquake and the torn veil that occurred upon Christ's death on the cross. That sounded scary, and if it sounds scary to me, who knows what a child would think of it? But I was willing to try on this journey for myself. I would be the scout. I figured Tain could attend the evening ones when he was older. I would definitely take him to the morning children's Good Friday service when school was out for the holiday.

That Palm Sunday I wrote in my Mass Journal: *What is the truth of my life? What does his sacrifice mean for me? He did not make me to only be about appearances and scratching for money. I must reach out, reach deeply and take back my life.* I can see I was still struggling with the issue of reclaiming my creative life. But I can also see that I had presented myself with questions to ponder throughout Holy Week. In this I am very much like Tain. I have my questions. What answers, if any, will I find?

On Monday night, I found the sanctuary lit only by candles for the Taizé service. This service is marked by the participants singing a kind of chant led by a cantor or lead singer. Its roots are in a monastic community based in France. At Trinity, the chant is led by a Taizé choir as well as by a cantor and accompanied by a few instruments, including a recorder and a cello. I realized I could pick up the chants without difficulty: the lyrics of each had just one line, and you sing it over and over. (One example was *Jesus, remember me when you come into your kingdom.*) That gave me plenty of time to catch on and eventually hit the right notes. The effect, I felt, was meditative and enchanting, as if the whole space of the sanctuary were a warm blanket wrapped around me. I found the words so comforting, especially the words of my favorite, "Ubi Caritas."

Ubi caritas et amor, Deus ibi est.

Translation: *Where charity and love are, God is there.* How true, I thought. How perfect.

I remember thinking, *here is another way to pray.* Ideally, we're to pray without ceasing. I can't remember where I first learned that, but I do know I wasn't sure how one put it into practice. Taizé showed me a possibility—you can pray without ceasing because you have something in your head that's like a pleasant version of an earworm. I love the idea: what if the song you can't get out of your head, the song you can't stop singing to yourself, were not some one-hit wonder from the 1980s but instead a short vocalization connecting you to God? Again, I felt comforted. I liked knowing I could call forth these short bits of words and music whenever I wanted. I chanted for over an hour, rocking gently in my seat and letting my voice rise and fall in step with the lead of the Taizé choir.

But I wasn't used to singing. The next morning, I woke up to find my throat raw and sore. Still, I drank my tea, drove Tain to school, then headed to Trinity for Morning Prayer at 10 AM I figured it would be low-key, something where I could be more of a spectator than a participant, unlike last night. As it turned out, I was right about the former, wrong about the latter. This service, I learned, takes place every week at Trinity, not just in Holy Week. It's usually observed by the church staff as a way to begin their week of service together. During Holy Week they are joined by a few others who, like me, have flexible schedules because they work from home or are retired. Mrs. Sutherland, the music minister, is one of the staffers—and that meant we did pick up the blue hymnal from the pew holder and sing. I did my best with my sore throat. I felt I had to at least try, because it wasn't a big crowd and it would be evident that I wasn't singing. Likewise, I spoke gently as I read the responses we made to the prayers.

The one thing I especially liked about Morning Prayer was this: we got to pick up the red book that sat next to the hymnal in the holder on the back of the pew, a book we rarely touched: *The Book of Common Prayer.* When my family first started attending Trinity I had picked it up, thinking it was a Bible. I couldn't tell what it was or why it was there, because we read everything for the liturgy from the printed bulletin the ushers handed us when we walked in. At Morning Prayer that day, I flipped through the red book while still trying to follow along with the service. From what I could glean it seemed like a prayer guide with practices and prayers that could be done individually as well as in church with the congregation. I made a mental note to explore the book further. First, I had to figure out how to get my own; I resisted the urge to borrow the one from my pew. On my way out, I shyly asked Pastor Kathie about the book and learned that copies are kept in the church library, and I could borrow one. I left happy, the red book tucked under my arm.

Then there was Wednesday and Tenebrae, which I approached with a certain amount of caution. I don't know why. I guess in these sparse settings and with the sparse attendance, I worried it would be too easy, and too noticeable, to do the wrong thing. But when I walked in the church I realized it didn't matter—it was so dark no one would really be able to see if I made the wrong moves. There was just enough light to see the program. The word *tenebrae* means "shadows" in Latin—hence the darkness. This is a service of shadows. It was even darker than the Taizé service because there were fewer candles and the church lights were dimmer. Near the altar were candelabras holding a total of fourteen candles. Throughout the service after certain readings a candle would be snuffed out, one candle at a time, until all had been extinguished at the end of the service.

I admit that when I looked at the candles and the program my first thought was, "Are you kidding me? All fourteen?"—yes, that long-service thing was still a bee in my bonnet. Isn't there any service in the Episcopal prayer book where you just pop in and pop out? I guess not. The lousy thing is I found myself focusing on the candles and not on the readings, most of which were strange and unfamiliar. One section of readings came from the Lamentations of Jeremiah the Prophet, and they were quite long. And they began with words I didn't understand:

> *Aleph.* How solitary lies the city, once so full of people! How like a widow has she become, she that was great among the nations!
> *Beth.* She weeps bitterly in the night, tears run down her cheeks; among all her lovers she has none to comfort her. . . .
> *Gimel.* Judah has gone into the misery of exile and of hard servitude. . . .[3]

The readings went on for two more sections like those, and then the reader sat down without putting out one of the multitude of candles. Pastor Kathie stood to recite something called the responsory, but I was thinking, *Wait! We don't get a candle extinguished after all that? This is gonna take forever!* Yes, this sounds as if I were six years old. Maybe I should have stayed home and gone to bed like Tain. The service went on like that: readings, psalms, responses, chanted antiphons. Finally, the last candle was extinguished, and we all stood to the sound of an antiphon: *Now the women sitting at the tomb made lamentation, weeping for the Lord.*

Pastor Kathie took the last candle, a single one, the Christ candle, representing the Lord, and put it behind the altar. Then more chant singing: *Christ for us became obedient unto death, even death on a cross; therefore God has highly exalted him and bestowed on him the Name which is above every Name.* Then Psalm 51, also sung, twenty verses in all.

> *Have mercy on me, O God, according to your loving-kindness;*
> *in your great compassion blot out my offenses.*
> *Wash me through and through from my wickedness*
> *and cleanse me from my sin.* (Ps. 51:1–2, BCP)

Pastor Kathie uttered a final prayer "for the gathering for whom Christ died." Then the sound, like a single loud thunderclap. The sound of stone against stone. Someone—it was too dark for me to see—brought the Christ candle back and placed it again in view.

At last it was over. Everyone departed in silence. I was relieved to be out of there.

I was tempted not to go back to church the next day for the Maundy Thursday service. I was tired of the mysterious experiences, and I knew there would be foot washing, but what exactly did that mean and how did it work without making a tremendous mess in the sanctuary? I went; I sat down and read the program and was comforted to see that the service was a pretty straightforward Eucharist with the foot washing part added in the same place where the imposition of ashes had been added on Ash Wednesday. At the end, the altar would be stripped and, like the previous evening, we would leave in darkness and silence.

I was hesitant to go up for the foot washing. Two chairs were on either side of the open gates of the communion rail; next to each was a stack of fluffy white towels and a huge ceramic white bowl with a large white pitcher inside. I still couldn't comprehend how it would work. And if I had let my mind remain caught up in the riddle, I suppose I would have stayed in my seat. But the words of the Gospel from John 13 broke me down. Because Peter tried to refuse when Christ went to wash his feet. Jesus answered, *"Unless I wash you, you have no share with me."* He gave them a new commandment, the heart of the Maundy Thursday service: *"I give you a new commandment, that you love one another. Just as I have loved you, you also should love one another. By this everyone will know that you are my disciples, if you have love for one another."* Something about this touched me, and I felt the ego and angst of my resistance. I wanted to step over that resistance, to put my vulnerability out there and allow my bare feet to be placed in a stranger's hands. And I did it.

When I think about this resistance now I am ashamed, especially when I see how, year after year, Tain is one of the first to leap up there and wash feet and get his feet washed when the time comes. When he attended the Maundy Thursday service for the first time the following year he took the Jesus doll with him. There's a photo of Tain with his legs outstretched and his feet over one of the big white bowls. "I got my feet washed and I washed someone else's feet, just like Jesus did," he wrote for the binder.

Pastor Kathie and the acolytes and chalice ministers removed everything from the altar: the cloths, the two candles in their wooden holders, and even the big gold cross that sits on a small shelf above the center chair in the nave. Then Pastor Kathie took the remaining bread and the chalice of wine, a small white cloth draped over it, and silently carried them to the chapel. This is where a rotation of people would sit through the night and pray, representing the hours Christ spent in the Garden of Gethsemane before his arrest. "Then he came to the disciples and found them sleeping; and he said to Peter, 'So, could you not stay awake with me one hour?'" (Matt. 26:40).

I decided my difficulty in letting go was something to contemplate when I returned later to sit for the watch. I had signed up for one hour at 2 AM The church isn't totally empty: the young people sleep overnight and have an evening of activities and prayer, and Pastor Kathie had made sure there would be at least one other parishioner so no one was serving the watch alone. I had planned to read through the book of John during my portion of the watch, but the room was lit only by candlelight and my tired eyes had trouble making out the small print of the Bible. I was going to pray or meditate instead, but my partner was talkative, perhaps to help himself stay awake. We ended up chatting through the whole hour. When I got home I went straight to bed so I could get up and drive Tain to the children's Good Friday service at 10 AM Darryl would be singing at the evening Good Friday service, so I didn't expect him to attend the morning session as well.

The watch was over, the young people who had stayed overnight had gone home, and Mrs. Vogelman had set up stations throughout the sanctuary. I noticed the wash basins and pitchers from last night's service were back and placed on the floor in front of the steps to the communion rail. The children's Good Friday service turned out to be my favorite of the week. A child's level was probably where I needed to be—where I felt I had a chance of encountering God during this consuming and confusing week. The service was designed to be a sensory experience, essentially an elaborate storytelling that would engage the children in the events of Holy Week, including the Passion of Christ.

Pastor Kathie, dressed in a plain black robe, started the story with Jesus's arrival in Jerusalem.

"We celebrated it this past Sunday. What was this past Sunday?"

Tain's hand shot into the air along with those of the other children. One of them called out, "Palm Sunday!"

"That's right," said Pastor Kathie. She continued this way, describing Jesus riding in on a donkey and the people waving palms. Every few sentences she would ask the children a question such as, "And what was everyone yelling when Jesus was on the donkey?"

"Hosanna!"

She explained how Christ and his disciples gathered for Passover and how Jesus instructed them to take off their sandals so he could wash their feet and why this was so important.

"Would you like to wash your feet too?" she asked. "Come on up!"

Tain popped out of our pew and trotted up to the basins. The children giggled as they struggled to pull off socks. Pastor Kathie and Mrs. Vogelman helped guide the pitchers so we wouldn't have puddles on the floor of the sanctuary.

Pastor Kathie then explained how the disciples were all washed and ready to eat and she talked about the Last Supper and how it is connected to the Eucharist we have each Sunday. "But for us today it's not wine; it's grape juice," she said. Tain's eyes widened and I heard his "Yay!" She blessed pita bread and grape juice and began handing it out. The Trinity Choristers, dressed in black robes like Pastor Kathie's, sang while she passed out the bread and while the children moved from station to station.

After their Eucharist Pastor Kathie walked the children, some of them still chewing their pieces of pita bread, to the back of the church and into the chapel. The parents all got up and followed and, for me anyway, made a delightful discovery. All of the Easter flowers for next Sunday's service had been delivered and placed on shelves, on chairs, and on the floor in this one tiny room. Flats and pots of lilies, tulips, hyacinths, daffodils, and pansies filled the whole space and transformed the chapel into the Garden of Gethsemane. It smelled heavenly.

Pastor Kathie told the children how Jesus had gone to the garden to pray and had asked the disciples to stay up with him and help, but they kept falling asleep. Then how Judas showed up with the soldiers who arrested Jesus. She led the children to the back of the church and talked about how Peter had denied Christ three times, and how the priests questioned Jesus before handing him over to Pilate. She talked about Pilate's encounter with Jesus and how he gave the people a choice about what to do with him. The children cried, "Crucify him!" and Pastor Kathie offered them a large bowl with water so they could, like Pilate, wash their hands.

The choristers sang a slow, dirgelike hymn, "Were You There When They Crucified My Lord?" and Pastor Kathie led the children to a large wooden cross on the other side of the sanctuary. With her help the kids lifted the cross and carried it down the aisle and up to the altar. They laid it on the steps where before they had washed their feet. They sat around the cross while Pastor Kathie told the story of the crucifixion. Then she led them downstairs to a space under the sanctuary where there's a kind of anteroom to the community room. The walls in this space are exposed stone from Trinity's original foundation, which makes it a perfect stand-in for Christ's tomb. After making sure everyone was in the room and that the smallest children were with their parents, Pastor Kathie had her assistants turn all the lights off for a few moments so the children could feel the silence and the darkness. I stood behind Tain, my hands on his shoulders. Everyone was so quiet. I almost didn't want to breathe.

When the lights came on again we walked out into the community room and formed a large circle. Pastor Kathie explained how she hoped all the children would help her on Easter Sunday to proclaim the risen Christ and say the first "Alleluia" of the season.

"Will you help me?" she asked. "I can't do it without you."

Tain nodded vigorously, and I promised myself we would get up early and be at the service in plenty of time so Tain would not miss the moment. This service had been brilliant, absolutely brilliant.

I loved the children's Good Friday service so much it emboldened me to take Tain to the Great Easter Vigil on Saturday night. The description in the Holy Week brochure encouraged us to bring noisemakers and food for a gathering after the service and I thought Tain would enjoy it, especially getting to stay up late. I was so excited for this I even tried my hand at making an Easter bread recipe I found that called for the dough to be braided and then colored eggs nestled into the dough before baking. I proudly left this offering on the table in the undercroft before Tain and I proceeded to the sanctuary. Darryl had arrived earlier because he was singing in the choir and was already in the choir loft.

But the Great Easter Vigil, as festive as it sounded, was not a great service for a six-year-old. It started at 8 P.M. in the dark— mysterious and fun at first, especially when he witnessed Pastor Kathie lighting a massive fire from which she lit the Pascal candle. As this flame was shared throughout the sanctuary, Tain was happy he got to hold a lit candle—a small white one with a plastic cuplike collar to catch the wax. Only the collar was not so great at catching the wax, which soon dripped onto Tain's fingers. He didn't like that. I managed to take the candle, but then I was holding two candles. This service, I know now, is akin to a long night of storytelling, relating God's works starting with Genesis. But it isn't the same kind of storytelling the children had experienced the day before. This was a lineup of adults reading long Bible verses. And I do mean long—soon Tain was leaning asleep against me while I tried to manage the dripping candles in my hands. I couldn't wait for it to be over.

I thought we would at least make it to the part where they turn all the lights in the church back on, proclaim the risen Christ and we ring bells and use all sorts of other noisemakers. I had brought a bell and Tain had a kazoo. When the burning candles spilled over and I got hot wax on my hands, I'd had enough. I blew out the candles, roused Tain, and we went home.

Our first Easter, I could have used a nap. We got up early—Darryl had to go practice playing trombone with the brass musicians who were accompanying the choirs for both services. I'd heard how people arrived early to get seats because the church would be so full and parents wanted to get good sightlines to take pictures of their children singing with the choristers. Once I made sure Tain was with Mrs. Sutherland and the primary choir, I sat in a pew and considered my job done for the morning. I wanted to just sit and listen to the beautiful music.

But Easter, I quickly discovered, is a bit of a raucous celebration at Trinity—nothing quiet about it. The sound of the brass, bright and sharp, bounced down from the choir loft, meteors of sound. Everyone in the sanctuary was saying "Happy Easter!" to each other. Right before the service began the primary choir, Tain included, sang "The Angels Rolled the Stone Away" and spun their wrists as they did so. Then two older boy choristers rolled a huge papier mâché "stone" down the aisle, and Tain and the rest of the Primary Choir joined them and rolled it back and forth. The adults laughed, took pictures and shot video.

I admit I was feeling a little overwhelmed as all this was going on—I guess I was just exhausted—because by the time Tain went downstairs for children's liturgy and a big Easter egg hunt, I was ready to fall asleep in the pew. But then Pastor Kathie began to talk about Mary Magdalene in her sermon, and I stirred. Mary Magdalene is my favorite of Christ's followers. I especially loved how Anne Bancroft portrayed her in the film *Jesus of Nazareth*. She was fierce in her love for Christ, barging her way into the house where Jesus was dining so she could wipe his feet and anoint his head with oil. She lied to a centurion and said she was part of Jesus's family so she could sneak up close and be near him under the cross while he died. She went to the tomb to anoint his body days later, and was one of the first to discover he was not there.

Pastor Kathie talked about the moment Mary Magdalene encountered Christ but didn't realize he was Jesus until he called her by name: "Mary." Suddenly I felt a strong desire to hear my name. Mary must have felt exhausted too—exhausted with grief and with love. It must have been such a relief to hear her name from a beloved's voice and to know at once that it was all worth it. I wanted to know that too. I wanted to hear my name. Pastor Kathie said there are some spiritual journeys that are intellectual, based on doctrine, while others are visceral, emotional, personal, and real. Was that what I had been doing all week long? Was I seeking the visceral and emotional? In saying her name, the risen Christ gave Mary that visceral experience, that sense of being known and recognized. Pastor Kathie said we long to be known by God, not as part of some grand connection to the cosmos, but as who we are as individuals in our lives and in our bodies. His grace travels to the most personal space in us, she said, engaging all our senses, and this is invoked by the speaking of our name.

Pastor Kathie went on to say that the communal experience of Jesus in our midst comes through the activation of our senses in the worship experience: the taste of the communion bread, the smell of the incense, the sound of a favorite hymn, the feel of being in a space infused with hundreds of years of previous prayers. She stressed that we needed to show up so our bodies can be reminded of Christ and so the experience is not just an intellectual one.

In the moment this made sense to me, but I didn't fully realize the truth of it, of how I had changed because I'd gone to church for eight days in a row. Until later that week.

Thursdays at Tain's school begin with a morning assembly with all the children gathered and seated on the floor in a beautiful round room with a piano and a small platform that acts as a stage. A couple of the classes present a skit or a report on a topic they have been studying, and parents are welcome. Singing is part of this, with the whole room chiming in on "My Country, 'Tis of Thee," "Simple Gifts" (the school's official song), and whatever cute season-themed song the music teacher is working on with the students. A handful of children stand on the platform and hold up big sheets of poster board printed with each song's lyrics.

I enjoyed these presentations and attended every week. Tain would come find me and give me a kiss on the cheek before leaving with his class to start the day. However, I never joined in on the singing. I don't know why. Maybe I thought I'd sung "My Country, 'Tis of Thee" quite enough when I was a kid and had to sing it each morning at my elementary school. Maybe, as at the church I had visited before Trinity, I was holding something back.

But that Thursday morning after Easter at Tain's school when the music began, I stood along with everyone else and I started singing. I was near the end of the song before I realized what I was doing. I hadn't thought about whether or not to sing, I just did it. I had acted from muscle memory, from what I had done service after service for those eight days: when you stand, you sing. And I liked the feeling when I did so—I could sense the communal spirit, of what it meant to do this one beautiful thing, whether each individual sounded beautiful or not, and to do it together. I knew that this was the way I would be from now on, an automatic participant in a corporeal body whenever it formed and gave voice. It was just as Matthew Kelly said: our lives change when our habits change. Because I had gone to church every single day for eight days, I was now a congregational singer.

When I walked back to my car in the parking lot that morning, I was already thinking about two ideas. First, developing some sort of daily prayer habit or ritual of my own, and second, developing one with Tain. We had both experienced the bigger realm of ritual. What would happen if we brought it down to the level of the personal?

I decided to start with the guide I'd discovered during Holy Week, *The Book of Common Prayer*. It has a section called "Daily Devotions for Individuals and Families," basically brief versions of the prayers from the Daily Office allowing one to observe periods of prayer morning, noon, and evening. But there were lines I didn't understand, instructions to use hymns or canticles I didn't know where to find. I went to the Internet and began searching daily practices even though I wasn't sure exactly what I was looking for. I came across a daily morning prayer podcast produced by a priest from an Episcopal Church in Maryland. It was a complete recitation of Morning Prayer, Rite II, including the day's appointed psalms and Bible readings. I listened and followed along with a *Book of Common Prayer* and a Bible in front of me.

The voice on the podcast sounded steady, warm, and friendly. "Grace to you," he began, "and peace from God our Father and the Lord Jesus Christ." And then: "The hour is coming, and now is, when the true worshipers will worship the Father in spirit and truth, for such the Father seeks to worship him." I felt hope and light in these words. Of course, these are pieces of Scripture— chosen opening phrases suggested in the BCP—but since I didn't quite know how this worked yet in the prayer service I flailed a bit, flipping through pages and trying to find where he was in the

Morning Prayer. But I figured it out, and from there developed my routine. After I took Tain to school I would sit in the meditation space, my iPod earbuds on, and pray this service long distance with this priest. I would pause it when he said the Bible reading so I could find the chapter and verse and read along, and also see where the readings fell in context of the whole story. Before I started going to church I wasn't a fan of prewritten prayers. I didn't understand why you couldn't just talk to God in straightforward conversation. But just as with the Taizé chanting, I discovered that repeating the same prayers daily allows the words to be carved into my being, words that I can call up as comforting mantras when needed. I especially loved and found inspiring the Third Song of Isaiah, *Surge, illuminare*:

> *Arise, shine, for your light has come,*
> *and the glory of the Lord has dawned upon you.* (Isa. 60:1, BCP)

One night while Tain was getting ready for bed I asked, "Hey, would you like to do Compline with me?" We had never done the "Now I lay me down to sleep" prayer when Tain went to bed, and yet I thought an end-of-the-day prayer seemed like a good place to start in helping Tain to create a prayer life of his own, to encourage him to talk to God in a way that makes the most sense to him.

"I don't know. What's Compline?"

"It's kind of like a little prayer service you do at the end of the day. You get to give thanks and pray for the people you care about."

He shrugged. "Okay!"

"You get into bed and I'll go get the book we'll use."

I retrieved the *Book of Common Prayer* from my office and joined Tain upstairs. He cuddled up to me and smelled of toothpaste and shampoo. I showed him where to begin and we read through the service together, choosing the shortest psalms when we came to them. When we got to the part that said *Silence may be kept, and free intercessions and thanksgivings may be offered,* I told Tain this is where he could pray for others. He lay back on his pillow and closed his eyes. He didn't raise or fold his hands, but his forehead seemed a little furrowed, as if he were concentrating.

"Tain, what are you doing?" I finally asked.

"I'm praying."

"Oh, okay."

I said my own prayers silently and waited. A few minutes passed.

"Are you done yet?"

"No."

"Okay, just let me know when you're done."

He nodded.

I was just beginning to wonder how long his list was and who exactly he was praying for when he said at last, "Okay."

I picked up the book again and we proceeded with Simeon's words.

For these eyes of mine have seen the Savior,
 whom you have prepared for all the world to see:
A Light to enlighten the nations,
 and the glory of your people Israel. (Lk. 2:29–32, BCP)

And then the final Antiphon before the conclusion.

Guide us waking, O Lord, and guard us sleeping; that awake we may watch with Christ, and asleep we may rest in peace. (BCP)

"Did you like that?"

"Yeah. It was kind of long, but I liked doing it."

"Well, it felt long because it was our first time doing it. It'll be easier from now on. Do you want to keep doing it?"

"Sure."

And so began our ritual. After several days, we moved it into the prayer and meditation space we have in our home. At first it was in the spare bedroom in a corner. I had bought red cushions to sit on and a wood chest from Pier One Imports on which I placed a statue of Buddha, an incense burner, a cup for water, and a small vase of fresh flowers (the water and flowers are offerings, reminders of life). When that room became an exercise room, I moved the altar into my office where it now sits with a set of Anglican Rosary beads and copies of the Bible and the *Book of Common Prayer*. Tain has always seen me sitting here, but usually it is in meditation.

This is where we did Compline for a time. Tain liked lighting the candle and burning the incense sticks I had there. I was glad he wanted to do these things because I wanted him to feel he can have a sense of the sacred anywhere, not just at church. He sat on the cushions and bowed his head when it was time for him to do his silent prayers. Then one night he asked if we could do communion as well. I hesitated on this and put him off by telling him we had nothing to represent the bread and wine. But really, I wanted to have time to look closely at what the *Book of Common Prayer* said about this. Was I allowed to give him communion? Was it something only a priest could do? From what I read it seemed okay for me to do. When doing the blessings, I just had to remember to say things like "bless us" instead of "bless you."

I bought pita bread and grape juice and Tain was thrilled. At first, I thought it was because he liked getting to have a snack before bedtime. He chewed noisily on the pita and drank the juice. "That's good bread," he said. But then there were evenings when we'd come home late after a meeting or a school event.

"You gotta go to bed, bud," I told him. "No time for communion tonight."

"But we could still do Compline."

"Okay, but you have to wash your face and get into your pajamas fast. No dawdling."

"All right!"

I loved having this routine for Tain and I was grateful for it every evening, while at the same time being sensitive to the fact that it might change or end completely eventually. The same could happen with my morning prayer. That's why it's good to have more than one way to be in relationship with God, because a method can become stale and rote after some time. But that is okay, in fact more than okay, because each time I can seek a new route of connection and the exploration will continue. Our practices ebb and flow and change over time.

■ ■ ■ ■ Tain's Take

Ten Places Where I Like to Pray

1. My bedroom. My bedroom is a very comfortable area. It is a nice spot to pray because it's private. Not many people come in when I don't want them to.

2. My mom's meditation station in her office is an area meant for praying. She has chimes that play when you pray, and you can burn incense and scented candles to help you relax.

3. The sanctuary at Trinity is an area that everyone is welcome to pray in. There are pretty stained glass windows all over the room that are nice to look at as well.

4. Outside in nature is very peaceful, and is an easy place to get to. I like to walk in the woods behind my house.

5. The guest room in our house is kind of like my room because I like to go in there when we don't have visitors. It is very quiet and comfortable and is a nice spot to pray. Plus, the window has a nice view. It looks out on the lilac bushes in our yard.

6. My living room is very nice and our sectional couch can fit a lot of people on it. It is a very nice spot to pray.

7. The library room in our house has a lot of our books. There are a lot of comfortable chairs in there and also it has a nice view of trees and bushes through the window.

8. The Johnson Room at Trinity is the church library. It is usually very quiet, and has nice places to sit.

9. The John Beach Room at Trinity is a meeting room but it has really new couches to sit on. It is also very quiet.

10. Pastor Kathie's office. Usually Pastor Kathie would be there to help me pray, and she also liked to pray in there with other people like me.

So from reading this list, it is kind of easy to tell that you can pray anywhere as long as you are comfortable and relaxed.

How do I know when a ritual has run its course? It's a bit cyclical. Early, as when Tain and I started doing Compline, then communion: the novelty carried us—the enjoyment of saying the same words. Then we made an added effort to hold on to the routine when life events got in the way. He would remind me or I would remind him to do our ritual, amending it if needed to get it in. This allowed us to continue. But eventually there came a night when we didn't do Compline, or communion, and we didn't remind each other. We probably did it a few more times, not consecutively, but we both seemed to know it was the beginning of the letting go. Only when that particular practice had run its course was there room for the possibility of the next ritual to unfold.

We never know what the next practice will be, but it seems to show up when we're ready. One day I went to a CVS drugstore to get a flu shot. Near the door of the in-store clinic was a rotating rack of books, and while I waited I perused its contents. They were all spiritual and self-help books. One section had books for children, and that's where I noticed a little red, white, and blue book with its title designed to look half like a badge, half like a postage cancellation stamp. It had a gold star, blue wings behind the star, and a motorcycle dirt bike on top of that. It was *One-Minute Devotions for Boys* by Jayce O'Neal, [4] and it featured readings for every day of the year. Each month had its own focus. January, for example, was about "What Smart People Do (Wisdom from Proverbs)," February was "Hugs and Stuff (Love)," May was about "Talking to God (Prayer)," and June was "Heroes of God (Big Players in the Bible and Their Lives)." The setup was the same as that of most devotionals: a piece of Scripture, a discussion of the theme of the reading, and a sort of prayer at the end such as *Jesus, help me to learn how to pray simply. Remind me that you love to hear from me. Amen.*

I liked how the brief observations were simple enough for Tain, then age seven, to read on his own, but they were still challenging. Even if he didn't get through the whole book, I could see him coming back to it in a few years and approaching it with new understanding. So, I bought the book, and Darryl and I presented it to Tain as a baptismal gift in late 2011. In early 2012, Tain and I developed a ritual in which he would read the devotional for the day as I drove him to school each morning.

At that point Tain owned a little portable DVD player, and he enjoyed watching films such as *Toy Story* or *Cars* during rides, so he wasn't always pleased when I had to remind him to read his devotional first. But he would pick up the book, take in the words, and say "Finished!" when he was done. Then we'd have a little conversation about what he'd read to make sure he understood it, and also so he could express thoughts of his own about the topic. After our talk, Tain would read out loud the prayer at the bottom of the page and together we would say, "Amen." This didn't take long, and when we had finished he could turn on his DVD player and watch his movie or show for our remaining time in the car. Some days it seemed we didn't have much to say about the reading. But then there were days when we would have a talk that would make me think, *Yes. This is why we're doing this.*

One February morning after his reading I asked Tain what he thought that day's devotional was about.

"Love lasts," he said.

I thought that sounded like he was only repeating the headline at the top of the page so I pressed him a little. "What does that mean?"

"Love never dies."

I asked him to read the whole page, prayer and all, out loud to me. The devotional explained, "You need to know this . . . *you are loved.*" And the prayer at the bottom of the page said, *God, I know I am young, but please help me to truly realize how important it is to live in love. Amen.*

"That's a really important message," I said. "Some people are afraid to love."

"Why?"

He said this with such wonder and surprise that it made me glance at him in the rearview mirror. I could see that he had thought we had finished and was in the process of turning on his DVD player. But he had stopped and was looking at me. I think he was actually shocked. He turned off the DVD player *and put it down*! He was waiting.

"Well," I told him, "people are afraid of getting hurt. They don't even say, 'I love you,' because they're afraid the person they love won't love them back."

"Whoa." Tain shook his head as if it were the most bizarre thing he'd ever heard.

"Sometimes that does happen, but that's okay," I told him. "Because the love is still there and it still matters. The hurt goes away, but like the devotional says, the love lasts forever. So if you love someone, family or friend, it's important to tell them you love them and don't be afraid. You love as much as you want, okay?"

Tain said, quite brightly, "Okay, Mama!"

He said this as if it were the obvious answer, the thing that made the most sense out of this puzzling riddle. He was so accepting of the idea, so willing to be fearless about love. I had been well into adulthood before I could accept the virtues of risking heartbreak. I tried to recall if I had ever felt as Tain did, and wondered if I had lost this feeling for love somewhere along the road, only to find it again. But then I realized it didn't matter. What mattered was that Tain was this way now, and it was my job to recognize it and help him stay in this loving flow even as he grew older and his experiences might lead him to feel otherwise.

We didn't make it through the whole year with *One-Minute Devotions for Boys*. With summer vacation and then Tain switching that fall to attend a local school, Sandy Hook Elementary, we no longer had our time together in the car, and I would forget to remind Tain to read the book. But I felt that was okay because the book had already given us so much, and, as I said before, I knew he would come back to it.

Right now, we're in a time of rituals that must be simple and quick. A couple of years ago, at the beginning of one September, Mrs. Vogelman provided the children with a "backpack prayer," a laminated piece of paper with a hole punched into the top and a string that could be used to attach it to a backpack. On one side was a red heart and a silhouette of Trinity's stone façade and the Newtown flagpole. "Trinity Church loves you!" it said. On the other side, this prayer:

> *Father please bless me as I carry this backpack to school each day.*
>
> *Help me to grow in wisdom and grace. Help me to always try my best and to be patient when something is hard. Watch over me Lord, and keep me safe. Grant me strength and courage to try new things every day. Help me to have fun while learning Lord, and remember that You are always with me. Amen!*

We have two copies of this prayer. One stays in one of the pockets of Tain's backpack and the other floats around our kitchen. Sometimes it's on the counter, sometimes it's under a magnet on the refrigerator, sometimes it's on the desk where Tain does his homework. I've had him say the backpack prayer out loud while waiting for the bus to come rumbling down our street, but I can tell he's beginning to outgrow it. We'll probably return to the devotions book soon. Tain and I have also been discussing setting up a meditation space of his own in his room, but he's not sure if he wants to move his carefully placed belongings. He likes the idea of having his own prayer space, though, so I know we'll eventually set him up somewhere. I'm curious to see what location he chooses.

I can't be sure what changes these habits or rituals forged in Tain over time. Such transformation overtakes in subtle ways; aspects of a person can be gently pulled apart and re-knit, and you don't know it until you act differently in a moment, as when I didn't realize I had become a congregational singer until I was already doing it. Tain's changes, I soon learned, manifested most at school. And I was concerned about this.

One day on our drive home, during our first year at Trinity, Tain told me his friend Jonah wanted to give up something for Lent but he wasn't sure what it should be.

"Really?" I knew Jonah's parents and didn't recall their ever mentioning going to church. "Does he go to church?"

"I don't think so."

"Why does he want to do it?"

"Because I told him I was doing it and he thought it sounded like a good idea."

"Okay."

I made a mental note to have a talk with Tain's teacher. Tain loves to talk, loves to talk about what he's doing; that has always been his personality. It shouldn't have been surprising to me that since we were going to church every week and he attended church school every week, he would talk about it. But at his private school his class was small, just ten children, and I didn't know if there were rules about religion in the classroom. I wondered if a parent might complain that Tain was proselytizing, and whether this would cause problems. Granted, I was probably projecting some of this concern based on my own wariness about religion when Tain first went to preschool at Trinity. I know I would have raised an eyebrow if Tain had come home wanting to imitate the spiritual practices of one of his friends.

A few weeks later I am visiting Tain's school for parent-teacher conferences, and while I'm waiting in the hallway I see that on the tops of their lockers his class has built a miniature town made of construction paper buildings. They've lined these up so it looks like a little Main Street extending all the way down the hall. While examining the town, I notice a red building with the words

"Trinity Church" carefully printed over the doorway. Part of me laughs with delight, part of me thinks, *Wow*, and part of me, I will admit, says, *Uh-oh*. Again, I wonder if this will cause any trouble. I take a picture of the building with my phone so I can show it to Pastor Kathie later.

"That was Tain's idea," his teacher said, when I asked her about it in our conference. "He thought the town should have a church."

"Is that all right?" I asked. I told her about Jonah wanting to give up something for Lent and how I was worried that parents might think Tain was trying to convert the first grade.

"Oh, it's fine!" she said. "He's not trying to make anyone do anything. He's just being Tain."

In the years since this conference I've had the opportunity to overhear some of Tain's conversations with his friends, and I've come to understand that Tain doesn't talk about faith as something others *should* do—he just talks about what he's doing, as he would with any of his activities. It could be as simple as what I recently heard him tell a friend while discussing video games: "I'm not watching Pokemon right now. I gave it up for Lent." But I've also observed these simple statements carry a lot of weight because of who Tain is. Recently I read a pastor's account in the *Forward Day by Day* devotional published by the Episcopal Church about how he's not interested in the debate on the public display of the Ten Commandments or prayer in public schools. He's more concerned with whether prayer and the commandments are on display in his life. Living demonstrations would affect way more people than anything written in stone.

I read that and wondered if that concept was at work with Tain in his first-grade class—and even now. The children Tain meets, such as Jonah, aren't necessarily looking to be connected to Lent, nor do they have an understanding, really, of what a spiritual practice is.

They are interested in Tain. They like Tain and he's nice, so their thinking could easily follow like this: If Tain is doing something— like observing this thing called Lent or going to church—then it must be a good thing because Tain is a good person. I want to try that. They are imitating behavior, as all kids do. And Tain is a role model. It is as if he is preaching the Gospel without using words— and I think that is pretty amazing.

Chapter 6

WHEN SUMMER DISAPPEARED

n June 2011, my family had been in attendance at Trinity for nearly six months. I was looking forward to the summer. Tain and I would have an open month to ourselves before his day camp started in July—because his private school year ended in early June while the public middle school where Darryl taught would stay in session well into the month because of all the snow days taken that winter. I figured this was a chance for Tain and me to try something new. I bought a copy of *The Connecticut Walk Book* and Tain's first pair of hiking boots. I thought we'd spend the time rambling through woods and discovering views from high hills. I was looking forward to our being together in nature.

That first Monday of his break, though, I'd hired a landscape firm to mulch the huge hillside bed in front of our house and I hadn't finished weeding it. As I was out there with the workers pulling weeds, Tain came out and asked if he could have a play date with his friend Thea.

"You can call her," I said. I'd been wanting him to practice using the phone more, to have conversations.

He went in but came back a few minutes later. "Maria wants to talk to you," he said.

"All right, I'll be right there." I pulled off my gardening gloves and went to our front door where Tain held the cordless phone for me.

"Sophfronia, Gian died yesterday," she said. "He was in a car accident."

"What?" I held the door open and looked out into the yard. I remember the sky being so clear and so blue, and the movement of the landscapers behind the row of our lilac bushes. How could the day look so normal? How was life still moving on? My mind flashed to a picture Darryl once took of Gian and me at the town's Labor Day Parade. He was telling me something and I was smiling, obviously enjoying what he was saying. I couldn't believe that would never happen again.

At first it seemed as if I couldn't hear anything else she said. Absolutely nothing. I think I was too focused on Tain, his face still so normal and expectant. How was I going to tell him? My brain kicked back in when Maria asked if Thea could come over and be with Tain because Maria felt it would be good for Thea. I thought it would be good for both children: I knew Tain would be devastated—he loved Gian so much. So I invited her to come right over. I hung up the phone and I felt as if I were caught in a horrible chasm. Tain was about to have his first direct experience with death, and my dearest friend had lost her husband. I was heartbroken because I had lost someone I cared about deeply, but I felt that there was no room for me to grieve because I had to be present for them both. I felt as if I didn't have room to cry.

I put the phone down and sat on our hallway steps.

"What did she say?" Tain stood in front of me and waited. I took hold of his hands.

"Tain, something sad has happened," I said. "Mr. Gian was in a car crash, a really bad one."

"Oh no! Is he all right?"

I held his hands tighter. My voice cracked with tears. "No. He died."

He let loose with a dual stream of tears and questions. "What happened? What will happen to Thea? Thea doesn't have a papa anymore?" I could only respond with my own tears and a stream that flowed with, *I don't know, I don't know, I don't know.* I hugged him. I felt paralyzed, blind, and dense like a stone statue sinking in a muddy pond.

Maria arrived with her sister Adele. The children occupied themselves in the yard. Honestly, I can't remember what they were doing. I think they were sitting on the swings on Tain's playground set and talking. All we could do was stand on the deck and cry. We said we would somehow get through this together.

I don't know how it occurred to me, but I managed to have one single clear thought that day: Tain should talk to Pastor Kathie. That was it. I didn't know what she could tell Tain, but I sensed this was the right thing to do in this vitally important moment. Maybe I figured whatever I said to Tain in the days and weeks to come wouldn't be enough. He needed to hear from more than one source. He needed to know he was not alone in this. Darryl agreed when I told him my idea, and I called the church: Pastor Kathie could see Tain in the early evening. When I told Tain where we were going, I could see he was confused. He probably thought it was something akin to going to the principal's office.

"It's good to talk to your pastor when sad things happen," I told him. "You probably have a lot of questions. And she can help you pray for Mr. Gian if you want to do that too."

Pastor Kathie's office felt like a little haven. She had comforting blankets and shawls draped over chairs, including a rocking chair, and a small sofa. There was a bowl of chocolates on the coffee table. Tain wasn't crying, but I could tell he was on the verge of starting again. I told Tain it was okay to cry, and that he could tell Pastor Kathie what had happened. I would sit in the next room, the church library, until their talk was over.

I was used to being in that room while waiting for Tain to finish choir rehearsal. I would peruse the shelves or thumb through the DVD study programs on the large rack in the back of the room. But that evening I could only sit there. I couldn't read, I couldn't think. I listened to muffled tones of Tain's and Pastor Kathie's voices coming through the wall. I couldn't hear what they were saying, but I sat there, just sat there, in the current of that sound.

When the office door opened, Pastor Kathie invited me back in. Tain was unwrapping a tiny Nestlé Crunch Bar and she asked him if she could talk to me privately for a moment. I sat down with my arms outstretched in front of me, running my hands over my knees. I felt cold. Pastor Kathie showed me *The Next Place*,[5] a children's book she had read and discussed with Tain. She asked how I was doing, and I realized I couldn't answer. I felt numb. She reminded me that I was grieving, too, and likewise had to look after myself. I nodded.

"Yeah, I'm working on that," I said. "Right now it feels like there's no room for my grief." And it felt that way, as if the grief of Maria, Thea, and Tain had to come first, whatever that meant. I know grief shouldn't have a hierarchy, but that's how it seemed to me. She reminded me again to take care of myself. We said a prayer together, then Tain and I left.

In the parking lot Tain said to me, "You're right, Mama, I did need to talk to Pastor Kathie. It helped. Now I know what to tell Thea."

"What will you tell her?"

"I can tell her that Mr. Gian is going to be all right."

"Yes, Tain. Yes."

The next couple of days are hazy, but I will try to draw them out of the fog of my memory as best I can. This has to do with my sister Theodora. I would say "younger," but since I'm the oldest girl in our family, all four of my sisters are younger. But Theo, as we called her, wasn't that much younger than me. She was born before I was a year old, so for about two weeks every year we were actually the same age—my Irish twin, as it were.

She held a master's degree in library science, and she worked as a student services coordinator at the local community college near where we grew up in Ohio. She was also our mother's attentive caregiver, and my mother and had moved in with her when Theo returned home after college.

My sister loved to cook, and at one point her weight ballooned to well over 200 pounds. I can't be certain, because I don't know all the details of my sister's life, but I felt the stress of being a caregiver was one of the roots of her health issues. Theo had bariatric surgery in 2004 and lost a lot of weight. In photos from our 2005 family reunion, she was smiling that bright smile of hers, and she looked healthy. But a few years later she began to gain weight again and suffered complications from the procedure. A few months before Gian's accident, during a family trip to Ohio, I had visited her and our mom and was shocked to find Theo bloated and unwell. My siblings and I had a conference call to schedule regular "respite time" when one of us or a home care aid would look after Mom so Theo could focus on herself. She arranged visits with her doctors and would call me late at night to talk about her treatment.

Theo said she needed surgery for scar tissue in her abdomen. The day we learned of Gian's death she went to the hospital for tests to prepare for the procedure. The following morning Tain and I went on a hike on a trail located in the woods a few miles down the road. I thought it would be good to get out of the house, and it would give Tain a chance to talk about the times he'd gone fishing with Darryl and Gian and how Gian loved to be outdoors.

My cellphone rang, and Tain went on a few steps ahead of me so he could scramble up a small incline. It was my mother.

"Theo went in for those tests but they kept her."

"Kept her? Mom, what do you mean? She's still at the hospital?"

"Yeah. They checked her in. I'm waiting to hear now. Vassie [my brother] is going to see about her."

I remember putting my phone away, stuffing my hands in my pockets and continuing the walk. I didn't know how to process what I'd just heard, but then Tain asked, "Who was that on the phone?"

"Grandma Ruby," I said quietly. "Aunt Theo is in the hospital."

"What's wrong with her?" He walked back to me on the trail and took my hand. We stepped on a series of rocks together and began climbing a hill.

"I don't know, Tain. I don't know."

When we got home, I called one of my sisters and learned that Theo's pre-op tests showed she had a severe pancreatic infection. Doctors were treating her, and all we could do was wait and see if her body could fight off the infection. I thought about how Theo had looked the last time I saw her. Could she fight? She had already been in such a weakened state. Tain and I went to see Maria and Thea that evening. Maria had begun to make arrangements for a service for Gian, and I let her know what was going on with Theo. She was stunned. I couldn't fathom Theo not making it, and yet I didn't know how she could.

Then the next day, another call came—this one from my brother Vassie. Theo's kidneys had begun to fail. The next twenty-four hours would be key. Our family members there in Ohio had taken up a bedside vigil.

The week before Gian died, before any of this happened, I had written in my Mass Journal in response to Pastor Kathie's sermon,

Pray so that Tain can hear me. Children get used to prayer when they hear us praying.

But in those hours and hours of waiting to hear if Theo would survive I could not pray.

I don't mention this now because I think I failed in this or did something wrong. It's just a fact. It is how I felt. I told Pastor Kathie this when I let her know what was happening with Theo, and she said, "That's okay. That's when you have other people pray for you." And that's exactly what happened. I knew she and other people at Trinity would be praying for us. I knew our names would be in the bulletin in the coming days, and we would all be included—my family and the Trottas—in the prayers of the people. But still I remember lying there in the dark that night and thinking specifically how that was a time when I was supposed to be praying but I couldn't do it. I was floating in a void, and I knew that soon this void would be filled with something. It was like waiting for something or someone to walk into a room. Nothing else could happen and nothing would matter until that star burst or that catalyst appeared. I waited.

The next day Theo died.

I went out to the backyard—to the area I couldn't afford to have the landscapers work on, and on my own I laid out thirty-six bags of mulch that day. I had to keep moving, or else I'd risk being buried in this fresh grief heaped upon fresh grief. I didn't tell Tain right away. I let him sit in front of the television, in earshot of where I was, because our family room opens up to this part of the yard. I could hear the cartoon he had on. I'm sure I got him food and drink when he asked for them. But for hours the mulching was all I did, all I could do. I couldn't tell him until I was able to stop moving, to sit with him. I had to be able to let my tears come.

I have pictures of Tain and Theo, taken the previous year at our brother's house in Ohio. They were dyeing Easter eggs and making faces at the camera. At some point I went inside, found those pictures, and sat down with Tain to tell him she was gone.

"What will happen to Maggie and Pepper?" He wanted to know about Theo's dogs—Maggie the black Labrador and Pepper, the old terrier who was diabetic and half blind.

I sighed. "I don't know, Tain."

We cried, but I think Tain was more concerned about me, in that I'd lost my sister. I'm not sure if he could process what the loss meant to him. When Darryl got home from school we discussed logistics. Tain and I would drive to Ohio so I could help my siblings begin to make arrangements. Darryl would fly out after he had finished the school year the following week.

Countless times I have driven the stretch of Interstate 80 that cuts horizontally across the state of Pennsylvania. From when I traveled it back to New York after my father died in 1991, I remember the smoky dark gray of the clouds as the road curved its way through the mountains, and the light snowflakes that I hoped would not get any thicker. When Tain and I drove to Ohio that summer day, I made sure he had all his favorite DVDs in the car, and I was careful to remember which exits had McDonald's along the way so we could have timely bathroom breaks and Tain could have a Happy Meal when he was hungry. I wanted to make sure the necessities were covered, because I knew my brain would be elsewhere.

What was I thinking about? Eventually, over the course of the next eight weeks, a sense of urgency would well up inside me. In July, Theo's birthday would arrive and then mine, and I would see how we would never again share an age. I would think about how time is not guaranteed to any of us, that our frail tether to life can snap at any time. I would walk through this grief bit by bit until I could wrap my hands around a figurative pickaxe, and start smashing my business life to pieces so I could make space to live a creative life again.

But all that was yet to come. For the hours I was driving with Tain to Ohio, I could only think about a number, seven. Whenever anyone asked, "How many kids are in your family?" I would always respond, "There are seven of us." There are seven of us, there have always been seven. "I have two older brothers and four younger sisters," I would say by way of providing detail. When I was in high school, my English class read a William Wordsworth poem called "We Are Seven," in which a traveler meets a little girl in her cottage yard by the road. He asks her,

"Sisters and brothers, little Maid,
How many may you be?"

She responds, "Seven are we," and goes on to list the whereabouts of all her siblings. Two of them "in the church-yard lie." The traveler is haughty with her.

"But they are dead; those two are dead!
Their spirits are in heaven!"
'Twas throwing words away; for still
The little Maid would have her will,
And said, "Nay, we are seven!"

This girl, the spirit of her, was in my mind as Tain and I journeyed across Pennsylvania. Something inside me kept asking, *How many are you? How many are you?*

And I kept thinking, *seven.*

We are seven.

Maybe I was seeking a miracle in this kind of mental math. Maybe I wanted to know Theo would still somehow be with us, that the number seven would be large enough to contain that kind of promise.

In grief, I tended to see the world around me shrink to a heart-crushing smallness. I couldn't think beyond the moment, the person, and the work that was in front of me right then and there. In this space, there was barely room to breathe. But I learned from Tain what an expansive grief can look like.

When we arrived at my brother Vassie's house, I helped Tain take his things up to the guest room where he would sleep. We had barely put down his bags when he saw there was a telephone in the room. He looked at me.

"Can I call Thea?"

"Yeah, sure."

I sat down in the window seat near the desk where the phone is and I watched him dial the number he knows by heart.

"Hi Maria, this is Tain. Can I talk to Thea?"

"Hi Thea. How are you?"

He listened. Then he said to her, "I'm in Ohio. I have to be here because my aunt died. But I'll call you every day and take care of you."

A knot of tears suddenly clogged my throat. When I took the phone from Tain to speak to Maria she was crying. She had heard him too. There must be room, I thought. If Tain could see it, could feel it, there must be room for all of this huge grief—room for our family and Thea's family and all my siblings—all seven of us. I found myself wanting to hear and believe in those words from the VeggieTales song, although the essence of them seemed so far away: *God is bigger than the bogeyman and he's watching out for you and me.*

God is bigger than this grief. God will uphold us all. I had to believe that. I had to remember it.

On my side of the family, Tain has a number of first cousins who range in age from adults to just a year or two younger than he. All his contemporaries attended the private viewing of Theo's body that we held at a funeral home in Elyria. My sisters and I shepherded the children down the narrow corridor and around the tight corners of the place.

When we came to the small room with Theo's open casket and a few rows of chairs set up in front of it, I recognized it as though it had always been present in a faraway corner of my mind. And really it had been, because this was the same parlor where, when I was about five years old, we had come to see our maternal grandmother after she died. I remember being lifted by someone to view her in her light blue nightgown. It had been nighttime, and I remember standing out in the parking lot with everyone afterward, waiting to leave. I had tried very hard to cry because I thought I should do what everyone else, the adults anyway, had been doing. I couldn't cry in the parlor, but for some reason, out there in the parking lot, the tears finally came. "I want Grandma," I had said.

That afternoon I was the one who lifted Tain so he could see his aunt's face one last time. Then we sat on the chairs, and Tain and I wrapped our arms around each other and just cried for a while.

"I'm going to miss her," he said. "And Maggie and Pepper will miss her."

"Yes," I said. "We all will."

As more family members entered, the sound of weeping increased, and it took on a singular essence—not like a song, but like many sounds becoming one voice, like those of crickets or peepers or birds. And the children seemed keenly aware of when that happened because all at once they wanted to leave the room.

"Can I leave now?" Tain asked.

The way he said it, and the way Tain and his young cousins left the room, was so matter-of-fact. They didn't whine or plead or anything like that. They had had enough of being in that room. They knew and had accepted what was and wasn't there: Theo was not there. There was a body and that was all. They went out and I went with them. They settled themselves on a sofa in a foyer and watched SpongeBob at low volume on someone's phone. Recalling how I had behaved at my grandmother's viewing, I was even more impressed by Tain and his cousins and their ability to stay within their own emotions. They did not take on the hard grief of their elders. Was it because they didn't want to or didn't know how? Maybe they simply didn't know any better—they were just being kids.

Tain kept his promise to Thea to call her every day. He left messages when he couldn't get her on the phone.

We stayed in Ohio for about ten days in all. Darryl joined us for the funeral and then a memorial service at the community college where Theo had worked. The school created a scholarship program in her name. My siblings and I, after several meetings, worked out a future plan for our mother that would involve moving her to the Washington, DC area, where two of my sisters lived. I made plans to return in a few weeks to help go through Theo's belongings at her house. Then Darryl, Tain, and I packed up and drove home to Connecticut.

We got back the night of June 29 and found two coolers of food, carefully packed, left by our deck door by our neighbors. I showed them to Tain, and we talked about how this is what it looks like when people show up for you, and how Pastor Kathie would say this is what faith looks like. I told him he was doing the same in the way he was showing up for Thea.

The next few days were harder than I expected, and I realized this was because we had lived in a kind of suspended state while dealing with Theo's funeral and, once we returned, Gian's memorial service. Though the grief remained, we had to get back to real life, but I wasn't sure what real life was supposed to look like. I wrote in my personal journal, *I'm feeling it's very hard to smile. I'm wearing yellow and orange so I have some brightness about me. I must find my way through this darkness.* I felt that I didn't fit into the world anymore because it was chugging right along, and

I wanted to do anything but that. I couldn't keep up anyway. I just wanted to sit in one place and heal.

Maria and I ended up doing just that the following week. When we dropped off Tain and Thea at day camp and went to the park to talk, we sat there for four hours without realizing it. That's how deep our grief was. That's how connected we were in it. We talked about how the mundane things in life—such as paying bills and filling out forms and doing client work—seemed so annoying and frustrating right then. We wanted dearly to focus on what makes life amazing. We wanted to think about what we could create, what experiences we could bring to our children. Also, I was angry because I felt the life I was living could not manifest what we were talking about. Anger, grief, and frustration tasted bitter in my mouth.

I think Tain also felt the awkwardness of trying to fit back into the world, because he had a tough time in those first few days of camp. He usually liked meeting new people, but right then there were too many new faces and too little connection. At least Thea was in the program too. They would need each other more than ever. And I recognized Tain would need more love and attention from me. On July 1, Darryl, Tain, and I went to see fireworks with a friend and her son and another little boy. We sat on top of her van and watched the exploding colors painting the sky. Tain kept quoting Woody from the end of *Toy Story*, the part where Buzz has a lit rocket strapped to his back, and he and Woody are zooming into the sky: "This is the part where we blow up!"

I quoted Buzz's response. "Not today!"

In church Pastor Kathie spoke of Paul and the struggle to do what we know is right, going against inclinations that can be lazy, undisciplined, unfocused. She spoke of the importance of spiritual connection and using that source of strength to help ourselves in a moment of choice to be focused and disciplined. Here's a note from my Mass Journal that day, July 3, 2011, which would have been Theo's forty-fourth birthday:

I am at war in my dreams and awake, trying to live in the way I know is right. The struggle is the same as St. Paul's. What do I do?

I must reach beyond my broken self. Find the solution rooted in my heart and spirit, not the problem. Rest in God's grace. Center myself in the spirit.

I wanted a big dose of faith, the warehouse store size—the kind of faith that makes you move first and ask questions later. I was in a fog. I didn't want to do anything. The only problem was, I knew the light of the Spirit was what I needed, and I wanted it more than ever. And what I wanted required action.

Small steps, I thought. I just had to figure out how to take a small step and figure out the rest from there. On my birthday a few days later I managed to take a step. I wanted to apply to graduate school for a master's degree in fine arts in creative writing. I was due in Virginia in a few weeks to help out with my mother, and I didn't know if I would have time to complete the application. But I decided to have faith and take one step, and that step would be ordering my college transcripts. That was enough just then.

I tried to focus on a dream I'd had a few years earlier but still thought about often:

I find myself walking through an old Victorian house. It's huge and beautiful, full of elaborately carved dark wood with stained glass windows and wide staircases. But the house is dilapidated. There's water pouring in through the roof and flowing down the stairs. The wallpaper is peeling away and chunks of plaster crumble off the ceiling. But I walk through the house happy and content, totally disregarding its condition because I'm reading a letter from God. My eyes are locked onto this letter; I can't stop reading it. The letter assures me I am loved. It's the most amazing thing I've ever read or felt, and I just want to focus on that—I know everything will be all right because of that. I just know I have to keep going. And I have to keep reading the letter.

Chapter 7

WHO IS THE TEACHER AND WHO IS THE STUDENT?

When our family started attending Trinity, we'd found a new community, yes, but we also delved each week into a sea of unfamiliar faces. I tried to attach a name to each face, but these details quickly faded and sometimes it felt as though I were starting anew. This is why it took me a few weeks before I realized Tain's church school teachers were not, for the most part, professional teachers. They were all parents, volunteering and serving in the church school ministry, often teaching their own child's class. Toward the summer the children's minister, Mrs. Vogelman, began recruiting the next slate of teachers for the fall. A grid printed in the weekly church bulletin showed each class, with its grade/age level and spaces for two teams of two teachers.

With teams alternating and the pair in each team trading off taking the lead, a teacher would only have to prepare and teach the lesson once a month; this was not an onerous commitment. As September drew closer I noticed in the church bulletin that a couple of the grid boxes for Tain's second-grade class were still blank.

"Do you want to do it?" Mrs. Vogelman asked me, when I inquired about whether she was any closer to finding names to put in those boxes.

"Me? But I'm still new here. I can't teach church school, I don't know anything." I wasn't kidding. And I wasn't sure how good I would be with a class of second graders. Over the summer, I had led children's liturgy twice while Mrs. Vogelman was on vacation, and I wouldn't call that experience a raging success. I sang terribly when leading the children in their opening hymn, and though Mrs. Vogelman had left the materials for each service, I didn't know the order of how she did things—when to light the candles, when to give the children their newsletter, or how quickly we had to move through everything before the acolyte returned to take the children back upstairs for the Peace. Fortunately, Tain was there to tell me what to do.

"Oh, you can do it, you'd be fabulous!" said Mrs. Vogelman. All I had to do was follow the curriculum. She would hold an orientation for the teachers and help us sign up for the Safe Church Training required by the Episcopal Church for anyone working with children. On Saturday mornings, Mrs. Vogelman would be in her office to help teachers plan for Sunday's lessons by suggesting books and pulling out materials for craft projects. I figured I could use the Saturdays to read and stay just ahead of the lesson plan. She was cheerful and confident, and I supposed I could just take my cue from her and be equally as confident. I said yes.

When I look back on this decision in view of what else was happening at that time, that wasn't a logical choice. I had organized an October live workshop event for my business; I had two ghostwriting projects for clients underway, and they were behind schedule because of the time I had taken to help with my mom;

and I had managed to apply to graduate school. On top of all this, Darryl and I were still trying to conceive another child, and I had gone back to the infertility treatments that had been interrupted by our summer of loss. Any one of these obligations would have constituted a full plate for me—or for anyone. But there I was, adding a responsibility that could have crushed me.

So why did I choose to teach church school? It was something like when Tain took ice skating lessons when he was five years old. I'd been fascinated with skating ever since I was a little girl watching skaters such as Dorothy Hamill in the Olympics. My parents didn't have money for lessons, so I had to wait until college where I took free classes Harvard offered its students. When Tain took lessons, I found myself sitting in the bleachers bundled up in my coat and gloves and leaning in so I could hear every word from Tain's instructor. My feet pushed against the floor as I automatically tried to mimic the skate strokes he was learning. Finally I realized how much I wanted to skate, and I changed Tain's class day so could I join an adult class that met at the same time at the opposite end of the rink from him.

After Tain's church school lessons, I had been asking him what he was learning, and I received answers that made me hungry to learn more. I had taken a few of the adult Christian formation classes offered at the same time as church school, but they only made me more aware of what I didn't know on a very basic level—especially since I wasn't "churched" as a child and I wasn't a "cradle Episcopalian," as a number of people in the parish were. So why not be in the room taking in the knowledge with him? And though Mrs. Vogelman didn't mention this specifically, it made so much sense that the church school teachers would be parents. It's another way for the children to take in the importance of what they're learning: it must be important if Mom or Dad is helping with the class, right? This was another way for Tain and me to share this adventure. We would grow in our faith together.

I wanted to do this well. Maybe I was overcompensating for what I thought was my less-than-scintillating leadership of children's liturgy, but I was careful with all the details in gearing up for church school. I attended the orientation, read through the curriculum workbook, consulted with my teammate and the other teaching team, and assembled the schedule so we would all know who was teaching what lesson and when.

On Saturday, September 17, 2011, I posted on Facebook: *At Trinity Episcopal Church setting up the 2nd grade classroom for tomorrow. It's my first time teaching Church School! I think my mom, who taught Sunday school for years, will be very proud.*

That morning I took Tain with me. Mrs. Vogelman showed us which classroom would be ours and explained what in the room belonged to Trinity Day School and shouldn't be disturbed. She showed which wall was ours to decorate, and assured us that whatever we put up would not be removed by the Day School. We were to take any supplies we needed such as markers, glue, construction paper, or craft kits, from the massive wall of plastic bins in her office. The first couple of months we would be learning about Old Testament people from the books of Judges and Kings. This part of the curriculum came with prayer cards not unlike the ones I remembered receiving at Fairfield Baptist Church all those years ago. I was glad to see them, and I wanted to make sure we used them. Each one featured the face of a person we would learn about—Esther, Ruth, Joshua, and so on. I created a row of these faces in a border at eye level near where the children would be seated so they could see and remember that we were talking about real people in all these Bible stories.

Tain helped me go through posters for the walls, and we chose colorful renditions of the Beatitudes, the Lord's Prayer, and Psalm 100, which I recognized as the "Jubilate" from Morning Prayer service. I figured we could read it out loud sometimes as an opening prayer. Once we had everything up,

I told Tain it was time to figure out what I was going to do for the next day's lesson.

"What's it about?" he asked.

I showed him the worksheet I would hand out and told how we would be learning about the book of Judges and a woman named Deborah who was a judge. She would sit under a palm tree and people would come to her with their problems.

"We should have costumes!" he said.

"Really?"

"Yeah! We can take turns being the judge."

"That's a good idea. What if we had a palm tree? You could be the judge sitting under the tree."

Tain's face lit up. "I think Mrs. Vogelman has a tree we can use."

He was right. She had a large potted artificial tree that would work for our palm, and she had costumes too—simple robes and headpieces that went on easily. Tain and I took everything back to our classroom. We set up the tree and organized the costumes and worksheets and the prayer cards we would hand out at the end of class.

"Okay," I said. "Looks like we're ready."

"I think so too!" said Tain.

The next morning Tain and I arrived a few minutes early. Church school was sandwiched between the two services, starting at around 10 AM I reminded Tain he would have to leave class a few minutes early with the other choristers to get ready to sing at the 11:15 AM service.

"Okay! Can I go get the snack?"

"Yes, but wait until Mrs. Wanzer [my teaching teammate] gets here. You can help her get it."

I smiled because Tain was buzzing as if the class were a party we were having at our house. I hung the clipboard with the sign-in sheet outside our door and Tain passed around cups and napkins to his arriving classmates.

The first few minutes of church school class, I've since learned, really is like a little party. It's our fellowship time. The other teacher and I ask the children about their week, what they're looking forward to. We hear details about vacations if they've been away. We talk about prayers that might be needed if a family member is ill or a test at school is coming up. I came to realize this is especially important because many of the children live in different parts of Newtown and attend different elementary schools of the four in the district. I wasn't tuned into this detail because Tain still attended the private school in Waterbury, and I thought he was the only one who might be a little out of the social loop. But most of these kids, not just Tain, didn't see each other during the week. Church school provided them with an important chunk of bonding time for their little community.

When it was time to begin class, I started with the phrase I noticed everyone at Trinity seemed to use at meetings and at the adult formation classes to get the room's attention and get things moving.

"The Lord be with you."

Thankfully, the children knew well the automatic response: "And also with you."

"Let us pray. . . ." And so we began.

The lesson went well. The children loved taking turns being "Deborah," even the boys, and judging on the issues their classmates brought to them. If I remember correctly, a number of the problems involved playground disputes. The only hard part, for me anyway, turned out to be Tain. He seemed less well behaved than usual, and I'm pretty sure this was because I was teaching. He wanted to show off that he already knew what we were going to do, and I had to ask him more than once not to talk while I was talking. Whenever the kids switched roles and changed costumes there was always a moment where Tain and a couple of the other boys would start roughhousing, and I had to get them to refocus. (The first couple of times I taught this irked me, but after discussing this with Darryl, who has spent his whole career teaching, I realized I had to keep reminding myself: these kids are seven years old. They aren't going to act like mini-adults. Yes, I had to maintain order in the classroom. But I could also know when to let go and enjoy their energetic ride.)

When it was time for the choristers to leave, Tain came to me and kissed me on the cheek.

"Bye, Mama! Good job teaching!"

"Thank you, Tain."

Four weeks later it was my turn to teach again. I had managed to pull off my writing and publishing workshop the week before—a full-day event with nearly fifty participants and multiple speakers. I'd spent the ensuing days following up with students and getting back on track with all the household duties I'd ignored, such as doing laundry. When Saturday came I was looking forward to having some quiet time to myself while I prepared for Sunday's church school lesson. Darryl made plans to get Tain's hair cut and run some errands. I bought a cup of tea from Starbuck's on my way to Trinity and sipped it while I took my time looking through children's books and thinking about what craft project to have the students make.

When I got home I barely had a foot in the door when Darryl, in the kitchen making lunch, said to me, "Tain's upset with you."

"Why? What'd I do?"

"You didn't take him with you to get ready for church school."

"What? I didn't know I was supposed to."

I went into the family room where Tain was playing with his toys and, sure enough, he was giving me the big-time pout. I sat down next to him.

"You left without me."

"Well, you and Papa had things to do. And I really needed to get the class ready, I just wanted to get it done."

"Yeah, but I wanted to help!" His voice rose and he was near tears.

"Okay, okay, bud. I'm sorry." I pulled him toward me and gave him a hug. "Look, I didn't know it meant that much to you. From now on we'll get the class ready together, all right?"

"All right."

"We'll go in early tomorrow and I'll tell you what we're doing so you'll know. Okay?"

He nodded. "Okay."

The next day in the lesson the class talked about Kings. Tain placed a plastic gold crown on his head and donned a purple robe with a black and white spotted fake fur collar, and stood modeling the role as we discussed what it meant to be a king. All the while I thought about what it meant to be teaching Tain's church school class, and this unexpected element of Tain's wanting to be so involved. I saw it all as a gift, a way for Tain to be engaged with his faith on another level. It wasn't that he hadn't been engaged before—and for all intents and purposes I was only teaching a quarter of his classes, so he still had to be engaged when I wasn't there or wasn't in charge—but now he was owning the process, the same way he owned the process of us coming to church in the first place because it was his idea. I knew the value of that feeling for Tain. I wouldn't take it for granted however and whenever that sense managed to develop.

▪▪▪▪ Tain's Take

used to really like church school. It was special to me because I could see a lot of my friends and talk about God. Another thing that I liked about it was that it wasn't too long. It was only about a half hour. Sometimes we would watch videos, and play games. Then my mom actually became a church school teacher. I liked this a lot because I always got to help set up and plan for the lesson. When I set up, I would get the crafts ready, get the snacks, and put on music. I really liked doing it because I got to spend time with my mom. I know that my mom liked this as well because this helped her get the lesson ready faster.

Now I don't have church school, but instead I am in the youth group. The youth group is like church school but it is for the middle school students. The youth group is really different than church school. We don't watch as many videos, or play games.

My mom is no longer a church school teacher now. She taught youth group for some older kids for a while and now she teaches the adult classes. In youth group, we talk about similar things that we talked about in church school. Recently, we talked about arguments and how to argue politely without hurting other people's feelings. The youth group has affected my faith because it has taught me more about God and kind things. We always have meetings where we do something nice for others, like sending out Valentine cards to college students, delivering pumpkins to people for Halloween, and even raising money for people during the holidays. I am looking forward to the things in youth group that we will do in the future.

▪ ▪ ▪ ▪

I was just plain grateful for Tain's help. He reminded me of how much the class liked hands-on activities, such as building a replica of the ark of the covenant as they did with one of the other teachers, and dressing up and acting out roles. I learned to look for personal opportunities to make the children feel the kind of ownership I sought for Tain, to know that they were a vital part of whatever aspect of the church or the Bible we were learning about.

I discovered this when we began a series of lessons about the Eucharist. As Tain and I purchased grape juice and pita bread for the class, I couldn't help thinking how funny this was: less than a year ago, Tain and I had experienced communion for the first time, with Tain's bad encounter with wine. Now here I was teaching about it. Here was another example of the unexpected turns our faith journeys seem to take. That morning I decided, instead of just talking about the Eucharist in our classroom, I would take the children into the sanctuary so we could talk about our actual experience of the sacrament each week during worship.

We looked at the beautiful kneeler cushions at the rail and talked about how the pictures stitched onto them depicted scenes from Bible stories. We talked about standing in line waiting our turn and what it's like to pray and hold out our hands for the Communion wafer.

"What's your favorite part of Communion?" I asked the class.

One girl chimed right up without hesitation: "I like it when Pastor Kathie says my name."

The other children nodded vigorously and began to voice their agreement. I had noticed that when she gave Tain a wafer Pastor Kathie always said, "Tain, the body of Christ, the bread of heaven." When I thought about it, I realized she did the same for all of the children, every single one, even the teenagers.

"Yes, yes!" The children were excited to discuss this aspect of Communion. Another girl added, "It's like she's saying a prayer just for me."

When I heard the girl say this, I thought about the dream I keep close to my heart, the one about the dilapidated Victorian house and my reading the letter from God. I also thought about one of my favorite Bible verses, in Isaiah 43: "You are precious in my sight and I love you." When I first read those words they, too, felt like a love letter placed in my hands, making me feel beloved and precious. I keep those words even now on the prayer altar in my office. I marveled at what I already knew, but seemed to be learning again—that we are all seeking to have a singular experience, a deep personal relationship with God. Our age doesn't matter, nor does it matter whether our journey is new or old. Of course this is what I wanted for Tain from the beginning. Now I was tasked with assisting his friends on the road as well. The little girl's words about Communion made me understand my role more clearly, and I hope I've been a better teacher for it.

One Sunday Pastor Kathie mentioned a session she would hold to discuss baptisms for those who wanted to participate in this sacrament in early November, for All Saints Day. She said you had to have six months of regular attendance, and I realized with some surprise that our family had already met that requirement. And even the aspect of baptism I'd been reluctant about with the Reverend Peter Gomes in college, about being an active participant in the faith community, was no longer an issue. Our family couldn't be any more in the mix at Trinity. Tain was officially a chorister, wearing the black robe of a novice and singing every Sunday. Darryl was singing in the Choir of Men and Women, and I was teaching church school. Also, it seemed that this community had laid its claim to us in the way it had gently, easily become the boat in which we floated when the seas had so suddenly turned rough that summer. We had received cards and phone calls, and people would approach us on Sundays to inquire about how we were doing in our grief. And I had accepted their reaching out to us when I had most wanted to withdraw into busyness and the whirl that accompanies a death.

I owe this to Tain. If I hadn't been committed to his presence at Trinity, I would have disappeared, at least temporarily. Instead, I accepted the well wishes of my fellow parishioners and was better off than if I had been alone and grieving. The balm of Trinity was on our skin. So why not make it official for Tain and me? I remember looking at the date in the bulletin for Pastor Kathie's baptism session, and it occurred to me: Tain and I could do this together. We could be baptized at the same time.

But there was still so much I didn't know. I shared this with Pastor Kathie when Tain and I went to the prep session.

Baptism is not about knowing everything, she said. The main thing is understanding the baptismal covenant and being committed to the ongoing spiritual development to help me fulfill it. She gave me a book about baptism and recommended I look through the section on baptism in the *Book of Common Prayer*. No one else had contacted Pastor Kathie, so it seemed that it would be just Tain and I who would be baptized in November.

She asked Tain a few questions. I was surprised at what he knew about baptisms, but then I'd forgotten there had been a baptism at Trinity right before Easter. The children would have discussed baptism in both church school and children's liturgy.

I began praying the Daily Office every day. I felt I had to get ready. But I also read material that said I didn't have to force my spiritual practice and do it all. One baptism guide beautifully described how I didn't have to swim, how that would be too much of a struggle—something I identified with because while I can swim, it is a struggle for me to stay afloat. It's not an activity I enjoy. But I also don't have to be absolutely passive and just sink, either. I can float—I can be one with the water and it can carry me. I was trying to have this float mentality with my ongoing infertility treatment. I knew Tain was praying for a baby brother—he had told me so. I prayed and I tried to envision my uterus smooth and unscarred and my fallopian tubes unblocked and clear. But I have learned that I can be praying for one thing and an answer comes for something else entirely.

This answer arrived in the form of a letter and then a phone call informing me that I'd been accepted into graduate school at the Vermont College of Fine Arts. VCFA is a low-residency program, which meant I would only have to be on campus twice a year for ten-day intensive residencies, one in the spring and one in the summer. The rest of the semester I would be working with a faculty advisor long distance on a study program we would have assembled during the residency.

The director of the program let me know that there was no room for me in the next residency, the one that winter. I would have to start the following summer in June 2012. I was so thrilled, I didn't care about the timing. In fact, the extra months would allow me to finish my client work so I could begin my studies with a clean slate. I would also have time to figure out how to pay for the program.

Then, in late October, they told me they'd had a cancellation. If I wanted, I could start with the winter residency. I wasn't sure. When I looked over the list of deadlines, I saw that if I accepted, I would have to submit work for the residency's workshop within a couple of weeks. I was already strapped for time. That weekend, in fact, I had to drive nearly an hour to Greenwich so I could attend the all-day Safe Church training. I responded to the director's email saying I would consider her offer. I planned to think about it on my drive to and from Greenwich.

That morning, I left home under a cement-gray sky. The trees still held bright autumn leaves. A few snowflakes, a strange surprise, fell throughout my trip. When the Safe Church training began, the other participants and I, our cups of coffee and tea in our hands, had to break away from looking out the windows at the increasing snow and wondering what it would be like by the end of our session. Within a couple of hours it was clear we wouldn't finish. Weather reports showed the snow only getting worse, and we all agreed to finish up the program and leave early.

I was driving our old Honda Civic, a car that was fuel-efficient but not great in the snow. Making my way back to the highway meant entering a kind of maze: some of the local roads were already blocked from fallen trees and downed electrical wires. Traffic was thick and slow. Darryl called more than once pleading with me to find a hotel and wait it out. But by then I was already on the highway, and I felt safer staying there. If anything happened, I figured it would be easier for help to find and reach me versus being on an unfamiliar side road somewhere. I would just keep moving slowly with the traffic.

Besides, I had company—sort of. I was listening to an interview with a woman named Janette Barber, a writer, television producer, and radio personality—and what she was saying captivated me. She was explaining how whenever any opportunity presented itself to her, she had learned to just say "yes" even if she didn't know how she would do what had been asked, such as being executive producer of a show she had pitched.

"Just say yes," she said. "You can figure out the rest later."

I could do that, I thought. In fact, wasn't I already doing it—for example, by saying I would teach church school without knowing if I had the time or ability to do it? I could say yes to starting graduate school six months sooner. I realized I simply needed to have faith—I had already made a few steps down this new path. I had to believe that, as the Goethe quote said, Providence would move with me, to help me continue. So I told myself that when I got home I would email VCFA's director that I'd be in Montpelier at the end of December.

It was dark when I finally pulled into our driveway. I couldn't make it up the hill to the garage because the Civic's tires would only spin in the snow. I parked at the bottom of the driveway and walked up to the house. Darryl and I were still talking when, less than an hour later, we lost power. It wouldn't return for over a week. Was this Providence moving or Providence laughing? I thought of the saying: *Man plans and God laughs.*

We slept a couple of nights in our freezing house. I wrote on a legal pad, working on the short story I hoped to submit for a workshop for my first graduate school residency, but I didn't know how I would type it up or send it. I hadn't even been able to send an email saying I would accept the offer. The storm had wreaked havoc on Internet and cellular service throughout the area. My sister-in-law Mershela, who works for a Hampton Inn in Ohio, managed to get us a room for a few nights in a Hampton Inn not far from Tain's school. This turned out to be a boon, because Tain's school had power and was in session early that week. I was so focused on getting the story to Vermont that I barely thought about the baptism day for Tain and me that was coming closer.

The day before our baptism the power returned. I was relieved we could shower at home. We had a rehearsal at church that Saturday with Pastor Kathie and our sponsors: our friend Rick, the one who had first made me aware of community at Trinity, would stand up for me, and our friend Francine would be Tain's godmother. Pastor Kathie walked us through the bulletin and explained the procession around the church that would take us to the baptismal font. (At Trinity, the font is in the front of the church, not the back, the better for all to witness the proceedings.) She also explained how all the children would come to the rail, essentially giving them a front row seat and their own special role in the sacrament. I liked that idea.

At the font, Pastor Kathie showed Tain the shell scoop she would use to pour water over our heads.

"I do it three times," she said. "Do you know why?"

"For Father, Son, and Holy Spirit," he responded without hesitation.

"That's right," she said.

I glanced at Darryl. I could tell he was impressed with Tain's answer, and I was thinking to myself, *How does Tain know that? I don't know that!* Part of me felt inadequate and unprepared, but another part of me recalled the Janette Barber interview. *Just say yes.* Figure the rest out later. I would find my way into fulfilling my baptismal covenant. And, really, I had one of the best guides walking with me—Tain.

When Darryl and I got married, I remember arriving at the door of the chapel on my brother's arm and being slightly shocked to see all the people filling the room. Yes, I had sent out invitations and knew at least in theory that people would be there. But I had been so focused on the personal aspect of the ceremony that it didn't hit home that others would be involved and play a role if only to bear witness to the event. I felt the same way about the day Tain and I were baptized. The worship service began as usual, and the usual number of parishioners were there. It didn't connect for me until we got to the baptism part of the bulletin and no one left the church that I realized our community was part of this too. At one point Pastor Kathie even asked, as part of the ceremony:

Will you who witness these vows do all in your power to support these persons in their life in Christ?

The response of the people: *We will.*

Let us join with those who are committing themselves to Christ and renew our own baptismal covenant.

"Our baptismal covenant," I thought. Tain and I were in a room full of people who, for the most part, were all likewise baptized. All of us—we were in this together. And we all held the same belief, a creed we declared in response to Pastor Kathie's questions.

Do you believe in God the Father?
I believe in God, the Father almighty, creator of heaven and earth.

Do you believe in Jesus Christ, the Son of God?
I believe in Jesus Christ, his only Son, our Lord.
He was conceived by the power of the Holy Spirit and born of the
    Virgin Mary.
He suffered under Pontius Pilate, was crucified, died, and was
    buried.
He descended to the dead.
On the third day he rose again.
He ascended into heaven,
    and is seated at the right hand of the Father.
He will come again to judge the living and the dead.

Do you believe in God the Holy Spirit?
I believe in the Holy Spirit,
    the holy catholic Church,
    the communion of saints,
    the forgiveness of sins,
    the resurrection of the body,
    and the life everlasting.

Will you continue in the apostles' teaching and fellowship, in the breaking of bread, and in the prayers?

I will, with God's help.

We processed around the sanctuary as the congregation prayed for us.

Deliver them, O Lord, from the way of sin and death.
Lord, hear our prayer.

Open their hearts to your grace and truth.
Lord, hear our prayer.

Fill them with your holy and life-giving Spirit.
Lord, hear our prayer.

Tain, wearing his tie and dark blue cardigan, looked happy to see the children come to the rail. His friend Thea had come for the occasion and was at the rail too. Pastor Kathie blessed the water and poured it in a long, flowing stream into the font. Tain stood on a block that allowed him to lean carefully over it.

Tain Elijah, I baptize you in the Name of the Father, and of the Son, and of the Holy Spirit. Amen.

Tain doesn't like to get water in his eyes, so Darryl was quick with the thick white towel to catch the tiny rivulets that ran down his temples.

Then it was my turn: *Sophfronia Marie, I baptize you in the Name of the Father, and of the Son, and of the Holy Spirit. Amen.*

The water ran off the top of my head and dripped into the font. I waited for the towel and was careful to stand up slowly so the water wouldn't run down the front of my dress.

We moved over to the altar, where we lit candles and Pastor Kathie marked the sign of the cross in oil on Tain's forehead and then mine.

You are sealed by the Holy Spirit in Baptism and marked as Christ's own for ever. Amen.

Pastor Kathie turned to the congregation. "Let us welcome the newly baptized."

We exchanged the Peace, and the children from our church school class came forward to present Tain with a special cross they'd made and covered in sea shells. We moved on to the Eucharist and the service finished as usual. But downstairs we were treated to cake, took pictures, and received more presents. Rick and Martha gave me a tiny silver trinity cross and, I was excited to see, my own leather bound, gold-trimmed copy of the *Book of Common Prayer*. Tain's church school classmates presented me with a thin gold metal bookmark imprinted with a verse from Romans 8: *And we know that in all things God works for the good of those who love Him, who have been called according to His purpose*. Darryl and I gave Tain the *One-Minute Devotions for Boys* book that would become a ritual for the two of us. We also gave him the rosary that Darryl's mother, Margaret, had sent for Tain.

But Tain's favorite gift he still cherishes to this day was a godmother—Francine. It didn't take long for Tain to happily co-opt the whole family. We had been friends anyway, even before any of us had children, and our boys had known each other since they were very small. But after our baptism, Tain called Nate and Ben his godbrothers; Francine's parents became his god-grandparents. Though he was closer in age to Nate (he was a year younger), he was closer as a playmate to Ben. Nate and Ben would come over and Nate would only want to sit indoors and read or sometimes join the boys at the kitchen computer if they were playing a game he liked. But Tain and Ben loved to be outside, jumping in piles of leaves or rambling through the woods.

The afternoon of the baptism, Pastor Kathie and the youth minister, Pastor John, came over to our house to watch football. We had snack food laid out—chips and salsa and drinks. Tain was in and out of the room, playing with his toys while still being part of the party. At one point he walked in with bread he'd taken from the kitchen, and he began handing it out to us.

"The body of Christ," he said with each piece. "The bread of Heaven." I looked at Pastor Kathie—was this allowed? Was it somehow sacrilegious? But she smiled as if it were the best thing she'd seen all day.

When I discussed this time with Tain he told me his baptism brought him closer to God.

"And it was probably the same for you," he said. "Right?"

It was. But when I think about my focus on the people around us that morning I suppose there is a difference between Tain and me: it seems I look at the world through the lens of sacrament— I'm looking for outward signs of the invisible, of inner grace. But for Tain it is all one, available to be seen at any time if your eyes are open. Nothing is invisible. I remember how he said he saw God at the post office—not invisible. God was that close.

I recognized a kind of disconnect in me. I had dreams about God loving me, and yet there was something I doubted about the world around me. I wondered: In what ways am I tethered to the world? In what ways am I tethered to God, marked as I am as his own? Maybe this was all because I was still struggling, and I saw a long eight weeks ahead of me. I just wanted the year to be over.

Chapter 8

WHEN THE PATH OPENS UP

I'd like to say life after our baptism was somehow different, glowing and holy. I'd like to say that Tain and I talked about it frequently right after we'd done it and what it meant. It's true that during that December we observed our first Advent as a family—I learned the time of Advent is about slowing down and preparing for the birth of Christ.

But it wasn't like that at all—there was no time to slow down. No time for contemplation. I kept thinking I would reach a point where I could slow down. I just had to do all this other stuff in front of me first. I used to run the 300-meter hurdles in high school, jumping over obstacles and seeking to reach the finish line. Clearing a hurdle is fast, rhythmic: kick the front leg up, jump, clear the hurdle, pull the trailing leg through. And it keeps going like that: kick, jump, clear, pull—kick, jump, clear, pull—kick, jump, clear, pull. Eventually, I round the corner, see the finish line ahead, and sprint until I cross it.

But after our baptism what lay ahead was not clear. It was more like battling through the levels of a video game with unexpected obstacles popping up and new skills to learn. I couldn't tell where it would end. After Christmas, I would be going to Montpelier for my first residency at VCFA, an intensive ten days of workshops and lectures. Upon my return, I would be responsible for a reading list and submitting twenty-five to thirty pages of critical and creative work to an advisor every month for the next six months. There was no end in sight.

I was taking an Advent "refresher" that Pastor Kathie offered on Wednesday afternoons. We had a book of daily readings by various authors such as Thomas Merton, Annie Dillard, Henri Nouwen, and Kathleen Norris called *Watch for the Light*, and it seemed that reading and discussing that book each week stood between me and feelings of stress. But I had to laugh when I read this in the essay, "To Be Virgin,"[6] by Loretta Ross-Gotta, a Presbyterian chaplain and author:

> What matters in the deeper experience of contemplation is not the doing and accomplishing. What matters is relationship, the being with. We create holy ground and give birth to Christ in our time not by doing but by believing and by loving the mysterious Infinite One who stirs within. This requires trust that something of great and saving importance is growing and kicking its heels in you.

Tain could do that. He seemed to be able to influence people such as his classmates by simply being. It all seemed to be one for him: faith, prayer, God, Christ, Spirit, were all rolled up into a little red rubber ball that he could take from his pocket and bounce expertly a few times before putting it back again. When I bounce such a ball the thing ricochets off the walls and I am grasping the air trying to re-capture it. Or worse, the ball magically divides like the brooms in *The Sorcerer's Apprentice* and they fly around me out of reach. If I can catch up, I think, I can be more like Tain. But real life doesn't work that way, especially at Christmas.

I had managed to submit my story for the workshop, but I still had four client projects on my plate and I was having trouble finding the words for them. It did feel as though I were waiting for the light. If I could breathe and hope and let go of worry, it might just come. I wrote in my journal, *Advent started this week and this week is about HOPE. With God, all things are possible.*

Maybe that's how we ended up doing all that we did do that season, because when I look back on it now I see how crazy it was—including a party for Tain that mushroomed into something larger than I ever imagined. In November Darryl performed a house concert in our home, and Tain had planned a room in our library where kids could play video games and eat snacks while the adults enjoyed the music. But no one had brought children. I consoled Tain by telling him we could have a small holiday party with a few friends. They could make gingerbread houses out of graham crackers and milk cartons and decorate them with icing and candy.

I really thought "a few" kids were all that would come. I thought six would be fine; three or four would be perfect. Fewer houses to assemble, fewer goodies to gather. I figured we wouldn't get many RSVPs because Tain's friends from his school lived a good distance away, and these kids would have their own parties or others that were closer to attend. As it turned out, Tain's place was where everyone wanted to be. With both second-grade classes plus Tain's non-school friends in attendance, we had a party of twenty on our hands. Darryl and I had to stay up late the night before, assembling the bases of the gingerbread houses and adding leaves to our dining room table so every child would have room to work.

The party went well. Tain was thrilled to have his friends around him. The children finished off the evening by asking (asking!) if they could remove the cloth cover from our piano and play it. They took turns playing the Christmas music they had learned in their lessons for their recitals. It was an unexpected and beautiful Martha Stewart party moment. I loved it all.

Afterward I wanted to sleep for twenty-four hours and I couldn't. My mother was coming to stay with us for Christmas for a week. Darryl and Tain were both singing in the choir for Christmas Eve and Tain for the Christmas pageant, so there were services and rehearsals at Trinity. I was teaching church school. There were presents to wrap and cookies to bake.

The frustrating thing was that saying "no" wasn't an option. I had taken all this on because I thought I could keep everything at an easy, doable level. But God seemed to be laughing at my best-laid plans: twenty children at a party instead of four; my mother needing to be wheeled through busy Manhattan streets before Christmas.

I love my mother, but taking care of her is physical and emotionally hard business. Then, she didn't have the dementia she has now, but she had weak legs and arthritis throughout her body, and she alternated between using a foldable walker and being pushed along in a wheelchair. When she arrived, I realized how much her physical state had changed since her last visit a couple of years before. We live on a hill, and navigating the steps just to get her in the house was tough on both of us. We had to double that work to get her upstairs for a shower and off to bed each night.

But I didn't want my mother to stay in the house all day. I figured I would just take her with me as much as possible. This worked, for the most part. I wheeled her into my church school classroom, and she got a kick out of overseeing my lesson. One day after school had ended for Tain, I got us all ready first thing in the morning and we drove into Manhattan to Macy's the moment it opened so she could experience Santaland with Tain for the first time.

But then an unexpected feeling appeared. Her being with me sparked resentment. I knew it was connected to Theo's death. I kept thinking about how the difficulties I was experiencing for only one week had been her experience for years. The thoughts drained my energy and I became short with my mother when I wanted to be patient and focused, compassionate and loving.

Grace came one morning when I was bathing her in the shower. Something happened that's hard to describe. I had turned on the handheld showerhead and was about to run the water over her shoulders when I was struck by a feeling of familiarity. It was as if I were suddenly seeing her shoulders as mine and her skin, which doesn't look like my skin, seemed like my own. I thought about how physically Tain has always felt to me like an extension of my own body because he emerged from me—that simple biological fact. I never had trouble clipping his toenails or, and I know this is gross, picking his nose because it didn't feel any different from doing the same for myself.

That morning when I was bathing Mom in the shower, I realized, perhaps for the first time since I had become a mother, how I am an extension of her. I had emerged from her body in the same way Tain had emerged from mine. This thought somehow relaxed me. From that point of relaxation, I could be more loving and good-humored with her. As I ran the loofah over her body I recognized that someday my body would be like hers. Things got better. Still, when Maria, Thea, and Maria's mother joined us for Christmas, Maria said I looked tired. And the way she said it, I knew she'd never seen me look that tired. She was right; I was exhausted, physically and emotionally spent. But it was okay. I felt broken—and hopeful.

When I finally left for Vermont after Christmas I was thrilled to have four hours in my car alone—four hours just to breathe and think. Four hours, I've come to understand, is the right amount of time. For what? For renewal, for healing, to begin to get my head back in the right place. I've never taken antidepressants or any medication of that kind, but it seems to me that a four-hour stretch of time either by yourself or in deep conversation (or even silence) with a friend is a powerful palliative. I first learned this by chance during the four hours I spent with Maria in the park after Gian and Theo died. I learned it again on my first drive to Montpelier under a low ceiling of clouds in late December. It's the only way I can explain how I went from the sheer exhaustion Maria recognized to being so awake and energetic on campus that the people I met felt impelled to comment on my enthusiasm.

"I'm just happy to be here," I'd say in response. "You have no idea how long it's taken me to get here."

This was my first time being away from Tain for ten days, but I soon realized this didn't bother me—that was an important piece of emotional information. When he was about two years old I traveled to Arizona on my own and rode my bicycle one hundred miles in the Tour de Tucson. Most of the time on the bike I kept weighing the value of being away from Tain. I told myself that if I ever spent such a chunk of time away from him again, it better be for a darn good reason. I thought about this before I left for Montpelier. Would I come to feel those ten days of residency wasn't a good enough reason? Would my energy for the endeavor drain away in sheer emotional exhaustion from all that the year had contained?

But the whole time, I only felt loved—loved by the divine. I went to Montpelier to talk about writing and I did. I thought I would find my little writing circle and I didn't. Instead I found a couple of friends who spoke in terms of light and spirit—conversations I never thought I would have—and they seemed to think I had important things to say about both. I didn't receive what I thought I wanted—I received what I needed. Only God can do something like that.

When I returned home in early January there was a full moon, one of the really bright ones that make the night look like daylight outside. I went out there despite the cold and took long walks during which I mulled over what had been given to me. When I think of my spiritual journey I'm constantly wrestling with the question of how much is "my work" and how much is the work of God or the universe. How much do I let go? I had gone to Vermont looking for "my people." My ideas about those people were very specific: I was seeking three or four classmates who were really committed to their work who might form a writers' circle with me. I thought we would push, challenge, and support each other as many great writers of the past have done. But I didn't find any of those people. Instead I found two friends, and the ground we were covering had little to do with writing. Yes, our conversations would eventually affect my writing—that seemed inevitable—but not in the way I had envisioned. I was humbled by the thought. I was grateful to the point of tears.

I thought about the place in *Harry Potter and the Deathly Hallows* where Harry saw his own father as a boy and noted he looked well cared-for, adored. Once, I had looked at Tain with this question. I had looked at his classmates at school. I had looked at children in stores. I had thought: *What does well-loved, well cared-for, look like?* But in the days after I returned from Vermont, I realized I could just look in the mirror. *I am well-loved*—just as the letter in my dream of the dilapidated Victorian house told me.

And then, as if it weren't clear, Tain reiterated the message. The morning after I returned home, Tain came into my room. He had been getting dressed but was having trouble fastening the button on his pants. I buttoned him up, then knelt down to cuff his too-long pant legs. While I was doing this he placed his hands on my head and said, "I missed your brown hair." I looked up at him and his eyes were closed and he was smiling. It was as if he were forming a memory or even blessing me. Then he opened his eyes and put his hands on my face. He was still smiling. I said, "I missed you too."

The following month Darryl's mother, Margaret, the grandmother Tain called "Hammie," died. When Darryl told Tain, he didn't cry. And I think this is because instead of crying they told each other stories about her, such as how she loved to take pictures, but sometimes her finger would cover part of the viewfinder. Even now when we see this in a photo we say it's Hammie's finger reaching down from heaven.

I wonder, too, if Tain took the death in stride because it was expected—she was in her eighties and had been ill, and he got to see her before she died. He has had friends lose grandparents. But I also wonder whether this third close death in less than a year had made Tain all too experienced. And he was only seven. Darryl and his siblings planned a memorial service instead of a funeral, and we traveled to Ohio in March for it. Before the service, we went to the cemetery, and Darryl showed Tain where Hammie's ashes are buried in the plot next to where Darryl's father is. We told more stories about her and laughed, and it just all felt right.

In the spring of 2012, we experienced our second Holy Week. We could enjoy this Holy Week without the bewilderment of first-timers. In fact, I loved observing Tain's comfort with the Trinity building. It had become a second home to him, and he and the other children moved through it with familiarity. On Palm Sunday, Tain and I were in the sanctuary between services, and he wanted to walk on the palms and examine the nave. I thought it was great that he looked so comfortable. I took pictures of him standing at the pulpit and then sitting in the large center seat with the huge wood-carved back where Pastor Kathie sits during the service.

"How does it feel sitting there?" I asked him.

"Like I'm king of the church!" he said.

The words seemed timely, because I could see Tain getting stronger and more assertive. Not long after that Sunday I had a parent-teacher conference with Tain's teacher and I was happiest to hear these two things: (1) On two occasions recently, prospective students visited the classroom. Tain was the only one, both times, to go right to the child, introduce himself, and offer to share his school supplies. (2) Tain will strongly, vocally, stand up for himself if something is going on where he isn't being treated well. I was especially glad to hear this because there was a situation going on all year long between Tain and a little boy named Joe. They'd been good friends since kindergarten, but for some reason that year Joe was having a tough time in second grade and this was manifesting in his treating Tain badly—picking on him. Tain's teacher told me Tain was good at telling Joe when he was acting unfairly. He would even refuse to play with him if it got to a certain point.

Then Tain's teacher said, "The strange thing is that Joe will often apologize, and you'll see him trying to hug Tain ten minutes later."

Ah, I thought to myself, *Joe knows, on some level, that he's having trouble behaving. He directs it toward Tain because he knows Tain is the one who loves him. He knows he is safe with Tain because Tain will forgive him.* I felt that was okay, and I had absolute compassion for Joe. But at the same time, I knew this meant it was more important than ever for Tain to know how to stand up for himself. He knows how to love, and yet he must know how to protect his heart and know, as we discussed when reading his devotional, that he can love even when his heart gets broken. I think this scenario will play out many, many times more throughout his life. I see Tain being wondrously prodigal with his love.

That spring I was at least three times as busy as I was in December. But something was different. Instead of feeling behind with projects and events barreling down on me like a boulder from an Indiana Jones movie, I felt on top of it all. Even more—I felt I could ride it out. The writer friends I'd made introduced me to new books, and I devoured them on top of the assigned fiction I was reading for the program. I hadn't known about such writing before. I read Gerald May's *Dark Night of the Soul* and then N. T. Wright's *Surprised by Hope*. The latter blew my mind with a discussion of resurrection I found particularly freeing. I took more Christian Formation classes at Trinity and discovered Rob Bell through an excellent video series called NOOMA. I learned of Frederick Buechner, who wrote spiritually in both fiction and nonfiction. Inspired, I wrote a short story about a woman during Lent struggling to accept the feeling of God's love.

All this created, again unexpectedly, one of those weird video game obstacles. This one came in the shape of a powerful desire to retreat from the world. I'd never felt such a thing before. I had been feeling I was very much "done" with the world, and I started conceiving elaborate plots of how I might cloister myself in some sort of low-residency convent. I would have been happy just to sit in a room with my stacks of books and read for weeks at a time. I didn't know what to do with this feeling. But then in late May, as if God knew I needed help with this, Pastor Kathie delivered a sermon on the desire to retreat from the world. Her timing, or perhaps the Creator Spirit's timing, was once again perfect.

As if reading my mind, Pastor Kathie totally called me on it. She said in her sermon, "The human spirit hungers for a way of being in community in a way that retreats from the clamor of the world." She went on to ask, wouldn't it be wonderful if we could just hang out with like-minded spirits in our cloistered corner and enjoy being in community? She said the apostles probably craved this as well, to be in a place where they could stay together and think about what they learned from Christ and not have to defend their faith. Jesus knew it would be difficult for them. The basis for Pastor Kathie's sermon was John 17:6–19, where Christ is praying for his disciples because "they do not belong to the world."

She pointed out how they do not belong to the world, but Christ makes it clear there is no escape from the reality of the world. Yes, you can enjoy the community you have with each other, but the community cannot abandon the world. Of course my question about this was, *How?* How do I not abandon the world when I would rather be gardening and taking Tain to school and reading and writing and exploring and having nothing to do with the outside clamor? Here was Pastor Kathie's response: "Live in the world without succumbing to the pressures of the world, without getting entangled." She said we must have strength, patience, and faith to live in the world but not be sucked in by it. She acknowledged that there would be times when we are exhausted with the world and are ready to be done with it. I was thinking, *That's me!!!* She also admitted it was tempting to live away from everything but, she said, it is not Christ's way. Again, she said, "Be *in* the world, not *of* the world." She said wisdom, justice, and mercy will prevail if it prevails in us.

I realized I could use the VCFA residencies already in my schedule for the next two years as these necessary times of retreat. I just had to be in a different frame of mind so the refreshment I gained from these retreats would be more enduring, leaving me more able to do what we are meant to do: love with abandon. I felt encouraged because Pastor Kathie's sermon showed me that God knows we must be in the world, knows intimately our struggles. He means for us to be here: "I have called you by name." In the same vein, he does not mean for us to be harmed or beaten by the world: "You are precious in my sight." We are given signs and help at every turn. We are put in the path of each other to love, inspire, and encourage each other whenever and wherever we need it most. Tain naturally knows how to do this. Now I am coming to it too.

Not long after the Beatles broke up, George Harrison bought an old monastery and renamed it Friar Park. He turned it into a home and fed off the vibration left from centuries of prayers and meditation by others. He woke early and meditated every morning. He took long walks on his vast property, which he was constantly improving by planting trees and other vegetation.

Some mornings I pretend I am George Harrison, walking my property, conversing arm-in-arm with spirit. What did he think about on his walks, I wonder?

They say meditation gives you a space of quiet in your mind so you can respond rather than simply react to what happens to you. This space allowed me to see clearly, and to make different choices. One morning before school when I was combing Tain's hair he asked, "Mama, when will you get a baby in your tummy?"

I sighed. We had discussed this so many times, but he didn't know about the many rounds of surgery and unsuccessful in vitro attempts. The fact was that my uterus was just too scarred both from previous miscarriages and likely from his own birth as well. But at that point Tain was too young to understand, and still held out hope of having a sibling, and I had taken to just saying "I don't know." I was a cauldron of many feelings, but chief among them was this: How do I teach my son to believe in miracles when I know he can't have the one he wants the most? Is it hubris to even think I know this for certain? I wanted to move on. In that moment I felt I could. I decided I wouldn't have any more treatments. Miracles aren't my business anyway. I would leave it up to God. I didn't want to disturb his hope, though, so I told him once more, "I don't know."

Not long after that, Tain said out of nowhere: "I want to try Sandy Hook School. I want to go to school with Nate and Ben [his godbrothers]." I was surprised and discussed this with Darryl. We could have waved this off, especially since we had made such financial sacrifices to keep Tain in the private school, which we loved. But I could see that Tain seemed so certain, and I stressed this to Darryl. We decided to wait at first and see if Tain would repeat his request, and he did. I went to his school and spoke to his teachers to make sure nothing was making him unhappy where he was. Finally, I took Tain to tour Sandy Hook Elementary. The principal, Dawn Hochsprung, met us in the office and walked the halls with us. I liked how she addressed Tain so directly, answering his questions about lunch and recess. She seemed to know this tour and interview was more for him than us. She showed him the ducks outside that made the schoolyard their home. He liked her right away.

"Do you think you'd like to go to school here?" she asked him.

Tain smiled and nodded, his head bouncing enthusiastically. I laughed because it was obviously a done deal.

That autumn, after his first day of third grade at Sandy Hook, Tain bounded off the bus and joyfully announced, "I saw Ben!"

Chapter 9

WHEN CHRISTMAS DISAPPEARED

look back on the Facebook posts from the first ten days of December 2012 and I marvel at how ordinary they are.

> *December 2: First day of Advent! Tain and Darryl are singing in the choirs, I'm leading the intercessory prayers, teaching Sunday School, and reading. Our family is lighting the first candle in the Advent wreath at the 11:15 service. Lessons and Carols start at 2. Truly a day of celebration. If you're around, come join us!*
>
> *December 9: Advent is a wonderful season!*

This post also has a comment I wrote in response to a Trinity parishioner:

> *Yes! Today in church school we read from Isaiah, listened to "Imagine," and the kids wrote down their imaginings of a healed, ideal world. See their thoughts on the poster in the hall near the class rooms.*

I loved teaching that class. It was the day after the anniversary of John Lennon's death, and it felt wonderful to sit there with a group of eight-year-olds listening to one of his songs and talking about its meaning. I wanted Tain and his friends to know they could imagine a world and make it happen. They wrote their ideas on worksheets that we glued to a bright swath of yellow banner paper. We affixed large plastic letters, IMAGINE, and illustrated the poster with drawings. Of course, being third graders, they wanted a world with no homework and lots of candy. But they also wanted no killing. And they wanted people to be nice to each other. I took pictures of the poster for Mrs. Vogelman, who liked us to chronicle our classroom activities for showing at the end-of-the-year church school celebration she organized each June. And I took them for myself because I wanted to remember what an ideal world could look like.

But did I recognize we were living it, that the ideal was already unfolding in front of us with each amazing event, each act of love?

> *December 9: Piano recital! Congratulations Tain, Nate, Ben, Lenie, all the other young musicians and their awesome teacher, Francine Wheeler.*
> *December 11: Meet a deadline, clean office. Meet a deadline, clean office. So it has been ever since college. The pattern continues today—cleaning my office.*

In that post I had downplayed a significant achievement. The deadline was the completion of my second semester of graduate school, and I had just submitted the first draft of a novel, something I had struggled to do on my own for so long. Maybe that was another reason I was so into the "Imagine" assignment—because I was deep in the thick of crafting the creative life I'd been imagining for years.

December 12: My big brother Vassie just called to say he loves me. Am I a lucky girl or what? #grateful, #loved, #appreciated

On the evening of December 13, a Thursday, I sat in the church library, across the hall from where Tain and the children's choir were practicing their Christmas music with Mrs. Sutherland. It was nice to just sit there and take a few deep breaths and not think about anything. I didn't have anywhere else I needed or wanted to be. I posted:

> *Listening to Tain and the rest of the Choristers rehearsing my favorite Christmas carol, "Oh Holy Night." Life is good.*

The next morning the ordinary continued, right up to my doing my bus run (I was working part time as a substitute school bus driver to help pay for graduate school) and afterward making the very ordinary decision to take our minivan to the shop for a small repair. I was sitting in the waiting room talking to a woman from our church—she was writing thank you notes while waiting for her car—when a woman walked in to say she had tried to pick up her daughter at the high school across the street for a dentist's appointment, but they wouldn't let her in. The sirens went screaming down the street minutes later. The ordinary had been interrupted—forever interrupted.

The messages appeared quickly—automated emails, texts, and voicemail messages from the Newtown School District telling us all the schools were in a lockdown position with no one allowed in or out of the buildings because of a shooting at one of the schools. The messages didn't say which school. I remember the first breaking news report flashed on the screen of the television in the waiting room. Reports of a teacher shot in the foot. That didn't sound right to me, so I called the school bus depot—I figured the radio system there had access to the same emergency channels used by the police and ambulances. They would know something real. My supervisor answered the phone.

"Okay, Sophfronia, stay calm," he said. "The shooting is at Sandy Hook."

Suddenly there it was—that gaping, soundless void opened up, the same as when I thought I had miscarried when I was pregnant with Tain; the same as when I waited to hear if Theo would pull back from the brink. It is an abyss separating the now from what comes next. But this time I didn't step into it prematurely and start grieving. And I didn't stand there voiceless and alone because I had remembered Pastor Kathie's words: *That's when you have other people pray for you.*

I called Pastor Kathie. She already knew what was going on and would soon be on her way to the school. I went home and got there just as Darryl called. He'd heard the news from his principal and was on his way home. I called my oldest brother, Vassie. We said a prayer together and stayed in touch throughout the morning. I turned on the television and heard the reporters spewing casualty numbers that seemed to change every few minutes. I turned it off again. I sat at my computer and sent emails to three friends chosen specifically because I trusted their spirituality.

There's been some sort of shooting at Tain's school. I'm calm but worried, scared. Place is surrounded by troopers and ambulance people. Roads are packed. Waiting here at home for news. Please, please send prayers. I know Tain must be fine and all will be well.

Then I waited.

How did I do that? I know that question, because I've heard it many times. And I can only explain it like this: there are many kinds of faith. One kind would have me praying in front of the meditation altar in my office or asking friends to open that channel of communication with the divine during a moment when I had no voice. This kind was about faith in life and about the promise I made to Tain before he was born, after grieving for him unnecessarily, thinking he was gone. I made a choice to maintain my faith in his life until somebody told me for certain it was time to do otherwise. That morning my mind was on living out that promise. I'm not saying it was easy, but that's what I was doing.

Sometime before noon I received a text from Francine. She had seen Tain with his class. Within a few minutes another friend called with Tain on the phone.

"Hey bud!" I said. "How are you doing?"

"Good!"

I listened for signs of tremors or tears in his voice but I heard none. The one word "good" sounded so like him that I didn't question him about what was happening. I said Papa was on his way to pick him up.

When Tain got home, I was struck by how, despite what he had experienced that morning, he still seemed to be in the flow of the ordinary. He said he was cold and asked for hot chocolate.

"We didn't get to take our coats."

"I know." I hugged him and rubbed his back. "We'll get you warmed up. You can stand in front of the fireplace and I'll make you some hot chocolate."

"When are Nate and Ben coming over?"

We were supposed to babysit them that evening so their parents could enjoy a rare night out. Since it was a Friday and not a school night Tain knew they would be able to stay up late. He had been looking forward to it for days.

"I don't know." I looked at Darryl and then at my phone in my hand. Texts from Francine and then Pastor Kathie told me Nate was fine but Ben was unaccounted for. The last I heard, David was checking the local hospitals to see if he had been taken to one.

"Tain, do you know what happened at your school today?"

He nodded. "Robbers broke into the school," he said. "The Army came to help stop them."

"That's almost right. A lot of people came to help. There were lots of people there, right?"

He nodded again.

"But it was only one person—a man who came into the school with a gun. Right now, we don't know everything that's happened, but a lot of people are hurt."

His voice dropped to a whisper. "I heard one of the kids say the principal died."

I squeezed Tain's arm. "Yes, that's right. She died."

Tain shook his head. "Why did the man do that?"

"We don't know, Tain. Like I said, everyone is still trying to figure it out."

"But Nate and Ben are still coming over?"

"I don't know. Let's get you some hot chocolate and we'll wait and see, okay?"

"Okay."

Tain sat at our kitchen computer planning the games he and his godbrothers would play, and the new levels on Club Penguin he wanted to show them. I thought about how on an ordinary day they would be arguing over whose turn was next and just a few minutes later they'd be laughing themselves silly because they were little boys.

Night fell. That's when the text from Pastor Kathie arrived.

I took the phone into the kitchen and showed it to Darryl. Tain, sitting at the computer, asked his question again.

"When are Nate and Ben coming over?"

I sighed and looked at Darryl. He stood with his arms crossed, his face knotted with sadness. "Tain, come here," I said.

I took his hand and held it in both of mine.

"Ben didn't come home from school."

"How come?"

"Because he got hurt really badly, Tain. He was hurt and they couldn't save him and he died."

Tain's face dissolved. His big eyes melted into thin lines and his mouth opened in an awful slow motion. At first nothing came out—only a horrible frozen silence as if his body couldn't figure out how to take in enough breath for the cry it wanted to form. When the sound finally emerged it rose from deep within his chest, a solid wail, harsh and raw. His tears flowed hot and fast.

"I don't want Ben to be dead!" He sobbed.

A 19-year-old boy, armed with warlike weaponry, blasted his way into Sandy Hook Elementary. Tain's godbrother Ben was among the first graders killed, along with the adults who tried to protect them that day.

As Tain cried in my arms I thought he would be angry too— why would I even be thinking about that? Because when Tain and I had talked about death before, I had always added that he didn't have to worry about it for a long time. Death was something adults contended with more than children, and he had seen that line reel out with the loss of Gian, Theo, and his grandmother Margaret. But now children had died, including a child he loved like a brother. I didn't know if he would see this as a betrayal of what he'd known, of what I had told him. Maybe, at his age, he didn't have access to such anger yet.

"I know, I know," I told him. "We're all going to be crying for a long time. We're all going to be sad for a really long time."

I put my hands on his face and looked into his eyes. "Tain, you're going to have to be really strong because you have to help Nate. Nate's going to miss Ben so much and you have to be there for him."

When his tears had subsided, he told me he didn't know if he could do it.

"That's fine, bud. You don't have to do anything you don't want to do." I made phone calls and prepared to leave for Francine and David's house. A few minutes later Tain, his face still wet with tears, said,

"I want to help Nate."

I thought about the harsh winter of the previous year and the old barns and sheds crushed by the weight of the persistent snow. In the aftermath of the shooting, it seemed faith collapsed in many hearts all over our town. *Why did God let this happen? Where was God in all this?* I heard the questions in homes and at the library, in stores and at church. But Tain doesn't ask such questions, and neither do I.

We seemed to sense instinctively that this is where faith comes in. I remembered attending a party in a friend's home a few years ago, and my friend's young son, a toddler, standing in the kitchen surrounded by all these tall adults who were like the trees of a forest. We must have all looked the same to him at his eye level because he could only see our legs. Still, he put his arms straight up;

that's all he did. And I was struck by his utmost faith that someone would notice and pick him up. His action moved me. It moved me so much that I wanted to be his answer. I went over to him and lifted him into my arms, knowing full well that for my trouble I would get a look that said, "Hey, you're not my mom!" He would probably start wailing then. But that's not what happened. Having reached the high ground he sought, he looped one arm around my neck and calmly surveyed the room.

In the crushing days after the shootings, when there seemed to be nothing but darkness, grief, and hordes of people and media, I felt as though I didn't have room to mourn. I couldn't process the loss of Ben or any of the souls that left the earth that day. One afternoon I lay on the couch and cried, but then Tain, seemingly out of nowhere, was at my side. "What's the matter, Mama? What's wrong?" As a mother, I recognized such a moment was a teaching moment, when I could share with him my grief and talk about our loss, but in that moment I was too tired.

"Nothing," I told him. "I'm just a little sad right now."

I wanted, needed, to be like that toddler at the party. I wanted to reach out and feel in utmost faith I would be picked up and held by somebody, so I could grasp a sense of myself again. But in a season when the worst had happened, how could I summon such faith again? Muscle memory or, perhaps more accurately, heart memory came into play.

That Sunday I taught my scheduled church school class for the third graders. The room was packed with children, more than the usual number, as well as their parents who stayed with them. A counselor stood by ready to help if a child felt the need to talk privately. I sat on a tiny plastic chair with Tain sitting next to me and I had a Bible open across my lap. I don't remember the specifics of that lesson, but the "Imagine" poster still hung in the hallway, and I knew the children needed to know the world they imagined is still possible.

Then it seemed the weather was willing to do the mourning for us. A heavy, heavy, rain that could only be seen as weeping—as if something wanted to melt all the memorial flowers, cards, and banners into pulp and send them flowing into the Pootatuck River. Pastor Kathie said faith is people showing up for you. I'd heard her say that before, but she would reiterate it many times in those days. Perhaps this is what Tain experienced. I now see I was acting out of having faith in his pain—similar to what I'd felt after his adenoid surgery. And this is what he needed. I suppose God had worked on me, opening my eyes and ears to what Tain was telling me, often without words.

Here's what I mean. Tain was getting dressed for Ben's funeral, looking at himself in the full-length mirror in my bedroom. He was quiet. Then he said this: "I want to wear pictures of Ben."

"Well, remember we're all wearing pictures of Ben."

I showed him the square badges a friend had made so we could tell who was family and to make sure we were all seated together at Trinity. We knew the church would be packed.

"No," Tain said. "I want pictures of me and Ben."

"Okay," I said slowly. Time was getting short. I was responsible for driving a van of family members to the church. But I knew this was a request that had to be honored.

I went to the kitchen computer with photos Darryl and I had put aside for the wake. I printed up two of Tain and Ben playing in a pile of leaves in our yard. I carefully cut them into squares and fastened them with tape and paper clips to Tain's vest.

"Is that good?"

He looked down at the pictures and nodded and smiled.

At the church whenever anyone asked Tain about the pictures on his clothes, he talked about how Ben was his godbrother and how much fun they had playing in the leaves.

We have three mementos from that day. One is a small lighthouse Christmas ornament from Pastor Kathie. She had gathered all the children at the front near the altar and spoke to them about finding the light in dark times. She told them of the many places they have available to look for the light, including in God, with Jesus, and in their families. The lighthouse, she said, would help them remember their friend Ben, who loved lighthouses. It would also remind them that the light would always be with them.

The next is Tain's copy of the funeral program. He'd carefully written his name on the front, something he'd never done before with a church bulletin, because he wanted to make sure no one took it by mistake. Inside, in the blank spaces labeled "Children's Art Pages" he drew a large striped, lighthouse. Above the lighthouse he drew Ben atop what looks like a cloud or an airplane. I eventually realized this was Tain's rendition of the picture of Ben on the cover of the program.

The third memento is a tall glass candle illustrated with this same picture of Ben superimposed over a Thomas Kinkade painting of tranquil seas. Tain placed it on the table by his bed, and it's still there today. I'm grateful Tain has these pieces of memory. I'm grateful for the voluminous tears we all cried during the service. I'm enormously grateful that I had not been in a mind so thick and clouded with impatience and grief that I would have told him, "You don't need that. I don't have time to print pictures." Or "Put that candle down, it's not yours." Instead my heart found its muscle memory and acted from a familiar place. It whispered a reminder to have faith in Tain's pain.

I didn't take Tain to any of the counselors or resiliency sessions made available to the families of our town. I thumbed through the many grief books donated to our local library, but none of them connected for me. The one I brought home for Tain, a journal in which a child could paste pictures and write about their lost loved one, failed to pique his interest. I know many parents will think that odd, but I can only explain I sensed aspects of Tain's journey would have to be uniquely his own, perhaps because it involved faith. He already had people all around him, myself included, who could talk to him about God and God's presence in all of this. But to truly believe, to feel hope and comfort and be upheld in his faith, I knew Tain had to feel it himself. To a certain extent, all I could do was listen.

One night I was putting Tain to bed and I asked how he was doing, how he was feeling about Ben. I wasn't sure if this was the right thing to ask, and I didn't know what he would say. But he looked at me, his large brown eyes wide with wonder.

"Mama, I just have the feeling I'm going to see Ben again. He's going to come down from heaven and he's going to be here with all of us."

Each week in our church we recite the Nicene Creed. The last line of it says, "We look for the resurrection of the dead, and the life of the world to come." A few months earlier I'd read *Surprised by Hope* by N. T. Wright, who describes how branches of the Christian faith have either downplayed or lost altogether the concept of bodily resurrection. Somewhere along the way the idea of leaving earth for a better place gained traction and the idea of God's kingdom being right here, right now, faded. I believe in the bodily resurrection. Tain's words that night told me he does, too, but he knows it without having read N. T. Wright. He knows it in a deeper way than I can ever comprehend.

"Yes," I told him. "I think you're right."

Tain's Take

After Ben's death, things were really hard for me. Like I talked about with Pastor Kathie, I was on a trampoline at the choir party, and every time I jumped I said, "My friend Ben was killed." This was good because I wasn't holding in the sadness. I was really upset about what happened to him. But one night, I had a dream. This dream was about Ben, and he was talking to me. We were just having a normal conversation in a white void. He asked me questions like what it was like on earth, how his family was doing, and how I was doing. I also asked him questions like what heaven is like and what does God look like. He told me that he wasn't allowed to tell me that, and I would find out for myself eventually. Then he told me that it was nice to talk to me, and told me to wake up. When I woke up, I realized that I had tears in my eyes. I knew that this was a very strange dream, so I went to tell my mom about it. She told me that it was a sign from Ben to say that he was doing well.

My friend Jane down the street brought me a lovely shawl knitted in a blend of soft colors—rose and peach, lavender and pale blues.

"This one reminded me of you," she said.

That's when I learned there was such a thing called a Prayer Shawl ministry, and the people devoted to that ministry knitted shawls and prayed over them all the while so there is divine spirit in every stitch. In the days after the shooting, I learned such ministries exist all over the country as they sent shawls to Newtown—so many beautiful shawls. I showed Tain the shawl Jane brought, and he asked for one of his own. So I took him to the room at Trinity where the shawls arriving there were being stored. He went through a number of them carefully before choosing a small one knitted in shades of light green and white. We chose one for Darryl, too, in brown and orange.

Tain liked to sit reading with the shawl wrapped around his shoulders. Sometimes he would have it draped over his head like a hood, the same way that Darryl liked to do with his, while they watched television.

I was thinking about Tain and his prayer shawl in early February when it was my turn to teach church school, and the topic for that week's lesson was healing. I asked him if it would be a good idea to talk about prayer shawls as a way of healing, and he agreed. On Saturday, Tain and I went to the prayer shawl room and took more than enough shawls for all the students and laid them out in an elaborate display throughout our classroom.

The next morning in class we talked about healing and the different things that can help us heal. I asked the children if they knew what a prayer shawl was. They didn't. I explained how they were made and how loving people sent them to places where healing was needed. Tain talked about his—why he had asked for one, how he used it, why he liked it.

"It reminds me of the people I love who aren't here anymore," he said. "It's like feeling a hug from them."

He talked about how warm and comforting his prayer shawl was and showed how he liked to sleep with it wrapped around him.

"Does a prayer shawl sound like a good idea?" I prompted.

"Yeah!" they responded.

"Do you think you would like to have one of your own?"

They nodded vigorously. I pointed out how all the shawls in our room were prayer shawls. They could pick out their own.

The kids took to the idea immediately, wrapping themselves in the shawls and asking if they could take one for a sibling. I said yes. This was what they were there for.

I would have considered the class done and successful but I had another surprise. I had asked Pastor Kathie to visit us and talk about the sacrament of healing, which was at that time offered weekly in a service on Wednesday nights. She explained it, and then she actually did the whole ritual for each child. She asked each one what or who they wanted healing for, then blessed them and anointed their foreheads with oil. When I look at photos now, I see how focused the children are on Pastor Kathie and on what she is doing—each wrapped in a colorful prayer shawl. The room had seemed soft and full of light. And there was hope—perhaps the most hope I'd felt in weeks.

Chapter 10

GROWING PAINS

On Halloween night of Tain's fourth-grade year, he trick-or-treated with friends on the streets of our neighborhood. The balmy weather allowed it for the first time in two years—no freak snowstorms to freeze out the fun. Carrying a camping lantern, I walked with other parents, chatting and enjoying the evening. Our neighborhood is one of hills and long driveways, so moving on foot from one house to the next takes a bit of effort. We parents stayed by the road at the bottoms of the driveways. At one point Tain came trotting down to me, his cardboard UNICEF box rattling with the coins he'd collected. One of his friends was complaining.

"She said I shouldn't be asking for money," he said. "She said it's taking too long and the money I collect won't be enough to help people anyway."

I nodded and started walking toward the next house. "What do you think about that?"

"I think even if I got a little bit of money it would help because other kids are doing it."

"Do you think your teachers would have you collect money for no reason?"

"No."

"Do you like doing it?"

"Yes."

"Then you keep doing it. Don't worry about what she says."

By the end of the night even I was surprised by how much Tain had collected, about $75. "Whoa!" he said, when we finished counting.

"That's a lot of money, Tain. Do you realize you wouldn't have it to give if you had listened to your friend and stopped collecting it?"

He nodded.

"So that's something to remember. If you feel something is the right thing to do, you do it even if your friends don't think it's cool or convenient."

A few days later, Tain mentioned another conversation with the same friend. This time he had questioned the wisdom of something she wanted to do and she had become angry with him. Tain told me, "She said, 'My mom says you act that way because you go to that church.'"

We are less than two years removed from a classmate of Tain's wanting to practice Lent simply because Tain was doing it. It seems this girl might be a harbinger of what's to come as Tain gets older.

Growing up is like slowly awakening from a long dream, and the rest of your life is about trying to remember the truth of it, because you have a sense that it is real on some deep level. You want to remember, because what you knew then is what you most need to know now.

As Tain stands on the threshold of puberty, I see new challenges to his faith as he seeks to reconcile what he believes with what he hears from his friends. I am wary. He comes home talking about what kids say on the bus. The children are older now, more cynical. They like to repeat, with precious little understanding, what they've heard from adults. The topic of death comes up often.

▪▪▪▪ Tain's Take

I don't usually talk to my friends about my faith. And they don't talk to me about their faith. This is because not many of my friends go to church. Only a few of them do. I also don't talk about it because some of my friends have different faiths than mine. One time in fourth grade I asked two of my friends if they go to church. They both said no. One of them even said that church is just something parents force kids to go to so they can dress up in fancy clothes. My other friend didn't like the idea of church either. I tried to explain to them about how that wasn't at all what church was, but they just didn't like the sound of it. I am not sure why this was.

Another time a kid and I were for some reason talking about what happens when you die. I said that you either go up to heaven or become born as a new person. He said that none of that was true, and that it is just nothing but darkness when you are dead. I found this strange because God is light. The kid then walked away looking a bit sad. I think he said that because one of his loved ones had just passed away. This could be what it is like for a child if they lose a loved one and don't go to church.

If someone you know dies, going to church and knowing God can actually be very good. It seems not a lot of kids are comfortable with church, but I think it could really help someone at a young age, especially after 12/14. However, some kids might not understand church. It took a while for me to understand everything. But I can understand why someone might not like church. Some kids don't like wearing fancy clothes or sitting in pews for a long time. But I like most things about my church. You don't always have to wear fancy clothes, and because I am in the choir, I don't have to stay in a pew. And I also love to sing! This is why I really like church.

▪ ▪ ▪ ▪

Recently Tain and I were having dinner in a sushi restaurant in New York City. He told me about yet another conversation among kids on his bus about what happens after you die.

"They say there's nothing afterwards," he said and he shrugged. "Everything just goes black." He stabbed at a piece of California roll with his chopsticks.

"Does that sound right to you?" I asked.

He shrugged again. "I don't think so."

I took a sip from my cup of green tea. "You know, there are a lot of stories of people who died but a doctor or a paramedic was able to resuscitate them," I said. "None of them said anything about everything going to black. In fact, it was just the opposite. They talked about seeing a bright light and having the feeling of leaving their bodies and being able to see everyone as they floated above them."

"Is that how they can come to you and make you have visions and dreams?"

I was using my chopsticks to mix a dab of wasabi into the shallow dish of soy sauce and I was about to say, "Yes, that's right." But something made me stop and look at Tain. He had put his chopsticks down; his hands were folded in his lap. I could see the depth of his question sitting in the slight furrow of his brow.

Finally I asked, "Who have you seen?"

He looked at me and said the name with a calm but heavy certainty.

"Ben."

"Where were you? What did he say?"

"We weren't really anywhere, we were just kind of floating in space. It was like he's been away on vacation and he was asking me how things are since he left. I told him he has a new baby brother."

"Did you get to ask him anything?"

"I asked him how it was where he is. He said it's really nice and he got to meet God and Jesus." Tain grew quiet. When he spoke again I could hear tears in his throat.

"I don't like to talk about it," he said. "It makes me very sad."

"How come?"

"I just miss Ben a lot."

His tears flowed fully then. I went to his side of the table and held him. I told him we all missed Ben, but how wonderful that Ben came to him, that he got to visit with his friend.

"And really, you answered your own question, didn't you? It doesn't all go to black. I think you knew that before. You really know it now."

He nodded.

"That's really amazing, Tain."

He nodded again and wiped his eyes. "Yeah. It's really good."

I'm hoping Tain will always have the awareness to ask questions and to see the answers when they come to him. I'm hoping he'll remember that even in darkness he can find the light, and that in the light are love and familiar faces. I'm hoping this knowledge will buoy him as he journeys onward, even when his travels take him over rough seas full of tears.

The hardest thing now is that the whirl of change within Tain is happening while there is also a whirl of change outside of him in the form of transitions at Trinity. Shifts in demographics and in the way people view the importance of religion and spirituality in their lives are affecting churches everywhere. So such transition is not unique to Trinity. But it's all new for Tain. The parish has committed to an ongoing self-examination to better understand who we are now and how we are meant to play a role in what God is doing, both in our community and in the world at large.

The number of children in the church school program has decreased as fewer children arrive to replace the ones who are aging out. Many of Tain's contemporaries are busy with other activities. On All Saints Day, there weren't enough older children to present the various saints to the younger kids in children's liturgy, so Tain took it upon himself to do them all. I stood where the costumes were all lined up outside the liturgy room and helped Tain change into each one quickly. I made sure he had the right index card to read from as he stood in front of the children and explained which saint he represented. In less than an hour he became, among others, St. Luke, St. Peter, St. Nicholas, and Martin Luther King, Jr.

After twenty years, Pastor Kathie has been called elsewhere, and so has Mrs. Sutherland, the music minister. When I saw Tain hugging Pastor Kathie at our last Christmas Eve service together, it occurred to me how much she has been a constant in his life for five years. I knew he would be upset at her departure. And he was sad, but he also showed a willingness to let her go, which impressed me. He seemed open to whoever would come to us next. Pastor Jenny, from Virginia, joined us the following spring. Her soft southern accent tells of her Georgia roots. I'm curious to see where Tain's journey with her takes him.

Experiments with new programs and mission projects have reinvigorated the parish. But some have found other changes— such as moving from offering two services each Sunday to just one—problematic, even unforgivable. I find this strange because for our family, it is a relief. We were stretched, with Darryl singing at one service and Tain singing at the other, while I served at the altar as an acolyte or a chalice minister. But some people have stopped coming. I was concerned about what Tain would think of this. I didn't want him to believe his faith life depended on who was at the pulpit or who was playing the organ.

■ ■ ■ ■ Tain's Take

A few days before Pastor Kathie had to leave, I had another important talk with her. This was a talk to help me remember some of the things that happened with us. Pastor Kathie reminded me of how I used to have so many questions about God that made her think about her own faith. She said that it was like a gift that I was in her life. She also helped me remember the talk we had about Gian's death. She reminded me that Gian had died around the same time as my Aunt Theo died. I actually had a lot of people die in a row. First Gian, then Theo, then Hammie (my grandmother), and then Ben. But then she told me about a Gospel story when two disciples are walking to Emmaus, and a third person walks to them. The third person is Jesus, but they don't recognize him. So Pastor Kathie told me that something different happens when we leave earth, like we get a new spiritual body. Sometimes, I think that when you die, you are born as a new person, but you don't remember anything from your past life.

Another thing that Pastor Kathie helped me remember was the day I got baptized. She said that we talked about what the water meant. We talked about it as best we could at my young age. She also said that during a worship service, there are a lot of things that God does to help us that we can't see. For example, we don't see the Holy Spirit flying all around us. But when we are baptized, the Holy Spirit enters us as a part of us forever. I know that this isn't a scary thing; this is a great thing, because you get to have a greater connection with God. It is God giving you strength to live your life as a Christian. But because we don't see this, we use water because you can see it, and oil because you can smell it, and we sing music because you can hear it. When Pastor Kathie explained this to me, it made sense, because all of these things can represent the Holy Spirit. I remembered the cross made out of shells that my church school friends gave me when I was baptized, and she said that her son is 24 and still has his.

Pastor Kathie and I talked about Ben's death. I remembered that I had had a dream about God, and I was talking to him while I slept. I asked him how Ben was doing, and told him to give me a sign. The next day it snowed. I knew that the snow was a sign. Pastor Kathie told me I was probably right.

This was the last time that I got to really talk to Pastor Kathie. She lives in St. Louis now. I know that I will see her again, and that we will be able to talk like this more.

I have recently met our new pastor, Jenny. I haven't gotten to talk to her much, but my mom tells me that she is excited to get to know me and said I seem like an interesting person. But I wonder what it will be like to have Jenny as a pastor. Ever since I have been at Trinity, I have always had Pastor Kathie. I know Jenny will be different. And recently there has been a lot of other changes at Trinity. A lot of kids have grown up, and there are not many younger kids. A lot of kids have left choir and Mrs. Sutherland moved to another church. Now Mr. Don does choir.

But I know that change will always happen. Like on one of my favorite shows, *Gravity Falls*. At the end of the series, the girl named Mabel is upset that summer is going to end and she will have to leave all of her friends and go back home, because she was only staying with her uncle for the summer. Her brother won't go with her because he is starting an apprenticeship with an author. She accidentally starts the apocalypse. (You may need to watch the show to understand why.) But during it, Mabel learns that change can be a good thing. And her brother changes his mind about the apprenticeship and they both go back home after the apocalypse.

This is sort of like what is going on at Trinity because a lot is changing. I know that when I get to talk to her, I will really get to know Jenny. And she will get to know me. And in choir, I have gotten to know Mr. Don a lot more. I had my first church service with Pastor Jenny, and it was very different. Now, before the children go down for children's liturgy, they go up to the altar and Jenny says a prayer for them. And she moved the announcements from after the sermon to the end of the service. This is a lot different than it was with Pastor Kathie, but I know that I will get used to the changes. I have gotten used to change before. It is hard, but after a while it feels all right. I don't think that this will affect my faith. Maybe Pastor Jenny will be able to help my faith grow by teaching me more about the things that Jesus did.

Tain encounters doubt, sadness, and fear in a different way now. It's more unexpected, as if he's walked around a corner to find a fog ready to absorb him. But he still comes to me when this happens, and I still have the blessed opportunity to remind him of what he feels, of what he already knows. We experienced such times even during the writing of this book. One day he came to me and said he needed help remembering the conversation he had with Pastor Kathie after Gian died. I reminded him that he could work with the transcript of the interview he did with Pastor Kathie before she left our parish. They had talked about that conversation then. I also gave him the children's book she had shared with him, *The Next Place*. He took the material and left my office, but not long afterward he returned in tears.

"That book made me sad," he said. He sat on my lap and put his arms around me. "It says none of what you are will exist. You won't see anyone's faces again."

I hugged him. "You're reading it differently because you're older now," I told him. "But remember it's only one person's interpretation of what happens when we die."

I took him to our shelves of books and found my copy of *Heaven Is For Real*,[7] one of the many books donated at our local library and offered to families for free in the wake of the Sandy Hook shooting. I showed Tain the back of the book, and explained how this four-year-old saw things he could not have made up, including his grandfather as a young man.

"He saw faces," I said to Tain gently. "And so have you. You have seen Ben."

He nodded, and I went on. "That was real, Tain. You know it was real. You already feel all of it—God and Jesus and the people you've lost. You just have to remember what you already know. And I know that's hard. People forget all the time because of what we see and read and what other people say to us. That's why you keep practicing and praying and talking to God. So you can remember."

A similar thing happened this year at children's Good Friday service. After the choristers sang "Were You There When They Crucified My Lord?" he came to me in the chapel and hugged me because this song, which he used to sing absentmindedly while playing video games, now makes him cry.

I notice Tain is taller than Pastor Jenny and towers over the smaller children when he joins them for Communion—he does this because he knows it is the one time he'll get grape juice instead of wine. I don't mind. It's like when I continued to carry him downstairs after he woke up in the morning even when I could barely lift him and his coltish legs hung down in front of my torso. I did this because I knew there would be a day when I wouldn't be able to do it anymore. There will be a day when Tain will attend the evening Good Friday service and sing with his Papa in the Choir of Men and Women. That time will come soon enough. Let him drink grape juice for now.

But I do think about how he reads things differently now. I suggested to him that now might be a good time to revisit the *One-Minute Devotions for Boys* book. It might help him with his impending teen years. At the very least it would give him conversation starters with Pastor Jenny. I also know it would help Tain to experience children of faith like himself beyond Trinity's sanctuary, and that's where Camp Washington comes in. It's a retreat center run by the Episcopal Church in Connecticut located on a bucolic preserve about forty minutes from our home. In addition to adult programs, the center features summer camps and, throughout the rest of the year, weekend retreats for children of all ages. Tain enjoys meeting new priests and getting to design the services with the other young people, including music such as Beatles tunes. With his school friends, Tain will, at the drop of a hat, extol the virtues of Chef Ben's cooking and the beautiful, clean cabins that are totally unlike the ones he's experienced as a Boy Scout. He never gives up hope that one of his friends will join him at Camp Washington; he's that eager to share the place with them.

We visit Camp Washington as a family once a month for a late afternoon program called Second Sundays. It usually features guest clergy who offer thoughts for reflection. Then we have Eucharist and a simple supper (which is why I can confirm Tain's assessment of Chef Ben's cooking!). At this point Tain has attended summer camp, a couple of retreats, and many Second Sundays. When he gets out of our minivan, I notice how much the place, like Trinity, has become his own. He runs ahead of us through the yard, knows the name of each building, and can tell you how to get to the lake that's down the hill and through the woods. He jumps up immediately if a priest asks for help with the Eucharist. When I see him like this I'm certain of one thing if nothing else: faith needs a home. I don't mean a place where you go to find faith; I mean a place where you go to nurture the faith already within you. It's as if Tain's faith is a gorgeous, vibrant plant growing within him. He brings it to a place where he can take it out and give it some light—on the fields of Camp Washington, or in front of the stained glass windows at Trinity.

It occurs to me now to ask Tain if he would like to create a prayer space in his room. I suggest we remove and donate the desk he doesn't use because he does his homework at the desk in the kitchen. He thinks it's a good idea. But I think he doesn't want to move things around in his room. Something tells me I'm going to find out some time soon that he has laid claim to a corner in our guest bedroom. As long as he uses it, that will be fine with me—even if I have to remind him from time to time.

The reminding works both ways. One evening while driving him to Boy Scouts I shared with Tain a disappointment I had experienced with my novel. I thought it was done but my agent felt it needed another revision. Tain only had time so say, "I'm sorry, Mama," before I dropped him off. But that night when he was getting ready for bed he came into my room.

"Mama, what do you think will happen with your book?"

"I don't know," I said. "I'll just keep working on it, figure out a way to fix it."

"I think you should pray to God about it," he said. He tilted his head to the side and looked thoughtful. "But it may not turn out the way you think. I asked God for a baby brother. I got a baby godbrother instead."

I nodded and hugged him. "I will do that, Tain. I think you're absolutely right."

Tain would like to thank:

Papa for helping me improve at everything I do.
Thea and Maria for being there for me.
Pastor Jenny for helping me understand God more.
Mr. Wismann for keeping the Trinity Choristers going.
Mrs. Sutherland for introducing me to vocal music.
Michael Unger for helping me grow as an actor.
Michael Baroody for starting NewArts.
Lloyd Kramer for filming "Midsummer in Newtown."
Braden Bergan for helping me during the filming of
   "Midsummer in Newtown."
Gil Simmons for being a good friend.
Mrs. Vogelman for teaching me about God.
Francine Wheeler for being my Godmother.

Sophfronia would like to thank:

Lisa Miller, PhD, who interviewed me extensively while writing her book *The Spiritual Child*.[8] Our conversations allowed me to articulate my thoughts about our family's faith journey. She was also the first person to encourage me to write this book.

Darryl, who has remained open to the adventure.

Pastor Kathie, for years of wisdom and support.

The Wheelers, for providing Tain with a godfamily.

Lloyd Kramer, for unwittingly asking the right question at the right time.

Wendy Barrie, who listened so well when we first met and spoke of the faith of children.

Phil Fox Rose, who acquired and edited this book for Paraclete Press. Tain and I are grateful that you saw the value in our story.

The fantastic team at Paraclete Press including Sister Antonia, Rachel McKendree, and Robert Edmonson who helped produce this beautiful book and have championed it so well.

Bart Geissinger and the staff at Camp Washington, who provide a loving space for all children of faith.

Chief Meteorologist Gil Simmons of WTNH-TV in Connecticut for being a wonderful friend and a role model of strength and cheerfulness for Tain.

Sue Vogelman, our former Children's Minister, for supporting so many families in their faith journeys during her years of service at Trinity.

The church school and youth group leaders at Trinity I've had the pleasure of serving with including Peter and Cindy Anderau, Rick and Mary Chamiec-Case, Lisa Irving, Erin Lutz, Anna Moses, Chrissie Pierce, Julie Pierce, Scott Rousseau, Judy Rowley, Ben Toby, Kara Wanzer, and Forry Weatherby.

The members of Trinity's Christian Formation Commission, including Dan and Lindie Bacon, Maureen Costello, Amy Dent, Jean Kreizinger, and Erin Lutz.

The multiple loving influences on my faith life including Jane Brady, Bret Lott, Frederick Buechner, Rob Bell, Gail and Vaughn Buffalo, Sue Roman, and the Brothers at the Society of St. John the Evangelist.

The members of our faith family at Trinity, especially the Reverend Dr. Jenny Montgomery, who is walking this current stretch with Tain.

NOTES

1   *Jonah 2:7, JB*   Scripture taken from *The Jerusalem Bible*, published and copyright 1966,1967 and 1968 by Darton, Longman & Todd Ltd and Doubleday and Co. Inc, and used by permission of the publishers.

2   *that indefinable air*   J. K. Rowling, *Harry Potter and the Deathly Hallows* (New York: Arthur A. Levine Books, 2007), 671.

3   *Aleph: How solitary lies the city*   *Book of Occasional Services* (New York: Church Publishing, 2003), 76.

4   *One-Minute Devotions for Boys*   Jayce O'Neal, *One-Minute Devotions for Boys* (Bloomingdale, IL: Christian Art Gifts, 2011).

5   *The Next Place*   Warren Hanson, *The Next Place* (Golden Valley, MN: Waldman House Press, 1997).

6   *"To Be Virgin"*   Loretta Ross-Gotta, *Letters from the Holy Ground* (London: Sheed & Ward, 2000), quoted in *Watch for the Light: Readings for Advent and Christmas* (Maryknoll, NY: Orbis, 2001), 97.

7   *Heaven Is for Real*   Todd Burpo, *Heaven Is for Real: A Little Boy's Astounding Story of His Trip to Heaven and Back* (Nashville, TN: Thomas Nelson, 2010).

8   *The Spiritual Child*   Lisa Miller, PhD, *The Spiritual Child: The New Science on Parenting for Health and Lifelong Thriving* (New York: St. Martin's Press, 2015).

Who We Are

Paraclete Press is a publisher of books, recordings, and DVDs on Christian spirituality. Our publishing represents a full expression of Christian belief and practice—from Catholic to Evangelical, from Protestant to Orthodox.

We are the publishing arm of the Community of Jesus, an ecumenical monastic community in the Benedictine tradition. As such, we are uniquely positioned in the marketplace without connection to a large corporation and with informal relationships to many branches and denominations of faith.

What We Are Doing

PARACLETE PRESS BOOKS

Paraclete publishes books that show the richness and depth of what it means to be Christian. Although Benedictine spirituality is at the heart of who we are and all that we do, we publish books that reflect the Christian experience across many cultures, time periods, and houses of worship. We publish books that nourish the vibrant life of the church and its people.

We have several different series, including the bestselling Paraclete Essentials and Paraclete Giants series of classic texts in contemporary English; Voices from the Monastery—men and women monastics writing about living a spiritual life today; our award-winning Paraclete Poetry series as well as the Mount Tabor Books on the arts; bestselling gift books for children on the occasions of baptism and first communion; and the Active Prayer Series that brings creativity and liveliness to any life of prayer.

MOUNT TABOR BOOKS

Paraclete's newest series, Mount Tabor Books, focuses on the arts and literature as well as liturgical worship and spirituality, and was created in conjunction with the Mount Tabor Ecumenical Centre for Art and Spirituality in Barga, Italy.

PARACLETE RECORDINGS

From Gregorian chant to contemporary American choral works, our recordings celebrate the best of sacred choral music composed through the centuries that create a space for heaven and earth to intersect. Paraclete Recordings is the record label representing the internationally acclaimed choir Gloriæ Dei Cantores, praised for their "rapt and fathomless spiritual intensity" by *American Record Guide*; the Gloriæ Dei Cantores Schola, specializing in the study and performance of Gregorian chant; and the other instrumental artists of the Arts Empowering Life Foundation.

Paraclete Press is also privileged to be the exclusive North American distributor of the recordings of the Monastic Choir of St. Peter's Abbey in Solesmes, France, long considered to be a leading authority on Gregorian chant.

PARACLETE VIDEO

Our DVDs offer spiritual help, healing, and biblical guidance for a broad range of life issues including grief and loss, marriage, forgiveness, facing death, bullying, addictions, Alzheimer's, and spiritual formation.

Learn more about us at our website:
www.paracletepress.com or
phone us toll-free at 1.800.451.5006

SCAN
TO
READ
MORE